T0196442

AUTOMATED SALES

AUTOMATED SALES

A Systematic Approach to Boosting Your Business

STEFFEN RITTER

AUTOMATED SALES
A SYSTEMATIC APPROACH TO BOOSTING YOUR BUSINESS

iUniverse books may be ordered through booksellers or by contacting:

iUniverse
1663 Liberty Drive
Bloomington, IN 47403
www.iuniverse.com
1-800-Authors (1-800-288-4677)

Because of the dynamic nature of the Internet, any web addresses or links contained in this book may have changed since publication and may no longer be valid. The views expressed in this work are solely those of the author and do not necessarily reflect the views of the publisher, and the publisher hereby disclaims any responsibility for them.

Any people depicted in stock imagery provided by Thinkstock are models, and such images are being used for illustrative purposes only. Certain stock imagery © Thinkstock.

ISBN: 978-1-4917-9615-3 (sc)
ISBN: 978-1-4917-9616-0 (e)

Library of Congress Control Number: 2016908777

Print information available on the last page.

iUniverse rev. date: 06/27/2016

CONTENTS

PROLOGUE

MY FIRST EXPERIENCE WITH STARBUCKS

> Organization is a means of multiplying the
> strength of an individual.
> —Peter F. Drucker

A while ago, I was on my way to Dusseldorf. Due to a slight train delay I had to wait in Cologne central station for almost an hour. Annoyed by the idea of arriving late, I felt the desire to have a cup of coffee in a quiet corner. Pulling my trolley case packed for a four-day trip behind me, I strolled through the concourse; however, none of the options appealed to me, and before long I found myself standing in front of the station.

I looked to the left where the stairs lead up to the plateau and the cathedral. On the left hand side of the entrance there was a tiny little café. Then I glanced to the right where the round, black-green logo couldn't possibly be overlooked. I went for the latter. Rolling in—I was at Starbucks—I was welcomed by an inimitable fragrance of coffee and three friendly young women behind the counter. I stopped in front of the first young lady to study the offerings displayed on a board hanging right above her.

Maybe I waited too long. She interrupted my thinking by asking in a succinct and straightforward way, "So?" meaning something like "Your order please. What would you like to have?" Still not being able to make a choice I answered, "One moment, please." Maybe the diversity on offer was simply too much for me.

Finally I came to a conclusion and ordered a latte macchiato with the intonation of someone who has made a firm decision. Nadja, as she was called, seemingly glad that I had made up my mind, immediately put forward another question: "M, L, XL?" When I gave her a puzzled look she repeated: "Tall, grande, venti?" When I still didn't react—in my mind I was somehow still in the train—she delivered her final blow: "Well ... the size!" I flashed back into reality and said "L, please." (By the way, I think most customers, when presented with three options, would go for the middle, though most of the time it's the least favourable for the customer as you get less value for your money, relatively speaking. Nevertheless you are happy: you neither spend too much, nor get too little of whatever you order. Companies and salespeople should pay much more attention to this customer bias toward the middle as they design their offerings.)

I thought that was it. But Nadja held my cup in one hand and a black marker pen in the other. She obviously wasn't ready yet. "Syrup?" I gave her another puzzled look. I wanted a cup of coffee, after all. Taking my head-shaking, slightly irritated glance for an answer, Nadja ticked the box for *no syrup*. "Extra shot of espresso?" Meanwhile I had mentally arrived in the here and now. I had braced myself for more questions and said "No" instantly.

There were already three or four customers standing in line behind me. I felt that we ought to come to an end. Nadja had a different take. She looked at me, holding my cup marked with *latte macchiato* in her hand. She went on the offensive, asking me "What's your name?" Now, this was getting weird. I wasn't used to introducing myself when ordering a coffee. Although the question wasn't intellectually challenging I was dumbfounded for a moment. Immediately aware of it, Nadja added: "Well, your first name!" The additional cue was helpful, of course, and I answered truly and obediently, though in a slightly inquisitive tone: "Steffen?" This seemed to be an appropriate answer. Nadja wrote it by hand on a sticker on my cup. I watched her with fascination. Now I had my Steffen cup. I felt reminded of a children's birthday party.

Nadja and I had chatted quite a bit. In a way, we had made each other's acquaintance. But now she handed my cup to a colleague and turned to the next customer. I had the presence of mind to take my trolley and follow my Steffen cup. The middle one of the three baristas looked at the cup, turned it around to see what was written on it and said, matter-of-factly: "Three euros twenty cents." That was short and to-the-point. I gave her a bill and she handed me the change—things happened so fast that I didn't even read her name. Then, I moved on to the next barista whose name I cannot remember either. She asked me to wait just a moment until my beverage was ready.

Suddenly I decided to use my waiting time to make a quick call home and keep everybody informed about where I was. No sooner thought than done! Some loving words: "... Train arrived late. Now at Cologne central station waiting for the connecting train ..." My report was interrupted by a shrill voice. "Steffen, latte macchiato!"

"Cologne central station???" There was a slight irritation on the other end of the line. Luckily I was able to clear things up. I was only at Starbucks. Still having some minutes left, I sat down. I watched the three baristas doing their job. Each had her clearly delineated task where every step had its purpose. The front-line service followed a systematic approach, and the process was well-defined.

The person in charge would always know who was the right person for each job. Barista #1—friendly, matter-of-fact and with a slight penchant for cross-selling. Barista #2—the same strengths as #1 for replacement reasons, with the additional qualification of "calculating". Barista #3—having the manual skills of operating the coffee machine, foaming milk and mopping the floor from time to time, or something similar.

The requirement profiles are much broader, of course. But the basic idea becomes clear. Which system, which procedure does your business use? Which tasks can be deduced from it? These are questions you may ask yourself if you are a salesperson, or a business owner. Precisely how do you proceed to achieve which result? Is your sales activity well organized, and, most importantly, is it organized in a simple way? Is there a system behind your work, or does happenstance rule?

In our modern world, automatisms provide a reliable basis for successful, sustainable sales. It is time for you to fully realize that selling can be smooth and easy. Sales can be automated!

I wish you happy reading and lots of valuable insights!

Steffen Ritter
Sangerhausen, spring 2014

1.

LIFE AT THE SELLING FRONT: THOUGHTS AND REPORTS

THE GOOD OLD DAYS

> Tempora mutantur et nos mutamur in illis.
> (Times change and we change in them.)
> —Sixteenth century

WAS EVERYTHING BETTER IN THE PAST?

Do you remember the smile on Mr. Johnson's face? Until a few years ago he travelled the country, always friendly, smiling and waving at you from miles away. He was always there for his customers, always on duty for his renowned contractual partner. How wonderful those times were! Salespeople were truly busy with selling. They listened to their customers, focused on their core business and spent most of their time out of the office.

If a salesperson did hang around in their office, which was often just a home office, hardly anything happened except for an occasional phone call or the daily mail delivery. Sure enough, even then certain administrative tasks had to be performed. Data had to be filed into folders that, over the years, started to fill huge cabinets. Everything was neatly arranged. Though growing in volume, it remained manageable.

The world outside the office was still whole and healthy, with the customer at its very centre. Once a sales conversation had been conducted, a contract would be sent out. The salesperson would bag his success by hand, adorn it with a stamp and dispatch it. Licking or wetting the stamp was a ritual in itself. Depending on salespeople's diligence, commission statements would fill many pages. They would arrive in the mailbox, where else?

THEN THINGS CHANGED ...

In the mid-1980s the mobile phone appeared, ending this peaceful idyll. Round-the-clock availability became the epitome of a new quality of customer focus. Just give me a call! Those taking part in the first technical experiments would carry a case of considerable size equipped with a handle and telephone receiver. For security reasons, today's airlines would probably bar them from being brought into the cabin. However, to this day, you will still encounter field staff affectionately reminiscing about their first Motorola "bone".

The late 1980s brought the fax machine into the office. Letters could now arrive at any time of the day. Possessing a fax machine put you in the front row. In the early 1990s, digital phone networks became universally accessible. Modern-style mobile telecommunication was born. The devices were getting smaller. Having been the privilege of the technically advanced sales representatives, they now became an essential tool for every field worker.

Around this time, fax machines and traditional mail began to experience serious competition. The e-mail, which first surfaced in the mid-1980s, now began its triumphant advance. By the mid-1990s the World Wide Web made the Internet accessible for ordinary users. At around the same time, various applications changed everyday office life.

NOT TO MENTION TODAY

During the first decade of the new millennium, customer management programs and various online applications underwent further fine-tuning. Mobile access to customer data and various applications became routine practice in the sales process. Social networks such as Facebook, Xing and Twitter started to gain ground in the workaday life of an increasing number of sales representatives during the second half of the first decade. It remains to be seen which networks will remain relevant in the long run, what kind of new networks will emerge, and which will disappear.

In the era of the smartphone, what we are carrying with us at all times is not only the capacity to receive and make calls, but constant access to all of our e-mails and the full range of our social media activities. It goes without saying that customer data is available as needed. At any time, be it 7.10 a.m. or 11.30 p.m., office time never ends. We are equipped for any contingency. Welcome, sales of the future?

DO YOU STILL GET ALONG?

Many things have changed in recent years. Let us suppose a sales representative left our world in 1980 and returned thirty years later. It would certainly take some time to explain everything to him or her. Although deals are still being struck by human beings—one of whom makes an offer that the other accepts—the details of the procedure have changed significantly.

In today's environment, if you do not organize yourself and focus your attention you will barely be able to see any customer, due to an overkill of multidimensional distractions flowing in from all sides. Communication and administration needs alone can be overwhelming. In order to perform any task there is a need for an endless stream of back-and-forth mails, fax and text messages, phone calls and sometimes even face-to-face conversations. All of which takes up maximum time. All of which is invariably urgent.

Many business people, salespeople and sales representatives have got used to leaving their offices in the evening with various tasks unfinished. More importantly, they end the day without a valuable, measurable and presentable sales outcome. Of course, there have been similar days in former decades too, but now they have become more frequent. Today it is much more difficult to work in an organized way and to focus on the core business of selling. To be able to do so you have first to organize everything else—or to ignore it completely, thus risking an increased customer defection rate. This is no way to achieve outstanding customer care and customer retention.

Unfortunately, as a rule, salespeople aren't good at organizing. On the contrary, true sales talent and professional administration capabilities often seem to be mutually exclusive. It is necessary and helpful therefore to create automation systems to take care of the bulk of those tasks that simply have to be done. Great organizing skills are indispensable for anyone who wants to succeed in today's world of selling. A systematic approach to selling is all about standard practices and automatisms. It's these practices and automatisms that have to be filled with life when working with customers in today's world.

How do you manage your sales process? How do you organize your process of working with customers? Are any of your tasks done in an automated and highly professional manner? How do you guarantee that you can devote maximum time to your core selling activities? How do you make sure that your sales process is running smoothly, practically by itself?

For starters, I'd like to take you on a tour of how salespeople, employees and customers think. Each testimony comes from a real person I have met in recent years. They are all unrelated to each other. By the way, those of you who more or less recognize yourselves in what is described on the following pages aren't by any means in the minority ...

HEADING HOME

A man too busy to take care of his health is like a mechanic too busy to take care of his tools.
—Spanish proverb

A SALESPERSON'S REPORT ABOUT THE END OF HIS WORKING DAY

It is late again. The evening news starts in five minutes. I won't be able to watch it since I'm still twenty minutes' drive away from home. Time to switch off and relax, which, as so often, won't be easy, with too many things still waiting on my to-do list. I completely forgot about Kruger who has been waiting for me to call him back since last week.

It is more or less the same story every day. Sometimes I wonder if things will ever change for the better, back to how it was in the past when the ringing of the phone was music to my ears because it might be a customer calling! Now each call is just a new task to add to my ever-growing to-do list—or underneath it, for that matter.

It's true that over recent years my customer base has largely increased. It all started at the kitchen table. Moving into my first little office made me really proud, and I now have a prime site next to the town hall. Well, it is a small town with not more than 8000 inhabitants, but nevertheless, building it all up from scratch has been no small feat, I should say. Yes, I like my job.

However, it cannot go on like this forever. Last month was my wedding anniversary, and I wasn't even aware of it until my wife gave me a queer look, as I was about to turn on the TV news. It was definitely too late for flowers! Though inexcusable, it was quite symptomatic of my running behind events in recent times. Feeling guilty for missing out yet again is becoming a normal part of my everyday life. I do not feel comforted even when people slap my back and congratulate me on my achievements. If they only knew …

I'll shut down my computer now. The 142 unread e-mails will have to wait until tomorrow. That is the ultimate motivation killer, anyway. As soon as you manage to empty your inbox it fills up again. Everybody puts you in the cc. The worst kinds of nuisances are people who send an e-mail only to call an hour later in case you haven't answered yet. I should probably send out-of-office notifications even while I'm in the office. Some people simply do not seem to realize that I am earning my living by selling stuff rather than by answering stupid mail. In any event, things have to change. Going on like this forever is not an option!

I am therefore going to turn on the answering machine, switch off the lights, and close the door. I am off for today!

OFFICE WORK ISN'T EASY EITHER!

> In a time of universal deceit, telling the truth is
> a revolutionary act.
> —Attributed to George Orwell

REPORT BY AN EMPLOYEE

I have been working with Meyer for twelve years. During the first years, work was real fun as there weren't that many customers. My boss would even have time for an occasional chat. Now, however, it is all chaos. Sure, we are successful—one of the top players I would say, residing in one of the best locations in town!

Now I have to go and do the daily shopping. Our office is open until 6 p.m., and the supermarket until 7 p.m. In the country distances are short, at least. Whenever I have to work overtime I have a problem. I have to call home and ask my oldest to go and buy the most needed things. Being twelve years old, he is already able to do that. Most people don't realize how much time and effort goes into all these little chores. As soon as I arrive home my second shift begins. Of course, the company must be taken care of, but life is more than just the company.

The bigger our company, the more tasks my boss puts on my plate, often without telling me how I have to go about it. "You'll master it", he would say before heading off to a customer. I call it working in blind-flight mode. Having more to do than I can possibly manage, I'm constantly lagging behind. In fact, my boss is in the same boat. From time to time he sends me an e-mail at nearly 11 p.m. That cannot be healthy. I do not read it until the next morning, anyway. We definitely need more hands. We have even talked about it, but nothing has changed since.

Our business simply needs more organizing. Everyone should know what he or she is responsible for and how everything should be done. It would be best to write it down. My boss is a passionate seller, but not a big organizer. Sales activities would certainly benefit from a more structured approach, something my boss doesn't quite get. Whenever things do not work out, he knows no better than to ask everybody to work overtime. I should try and convince him that this cannot be a long-term solution. Let's see if it works.

It's time to leave the office.

WHO ON EARTH IS SMITH?

> You see, but you do not observe.
> —Sherlock Holmes

THE CLASS A CUSTOMER

It is 3.27 a.m. You wake up thinking of Smith. Does that sound familiar? You wanted to call him but then forgot about it. It wasn't the first time, and nothing to be proud of. Smith is one of the customers you have been putting off for five weeks now.

It's quite a challenge to find enough time for all those things you must, should, or want to do. You should bring in customers—good customers. By the way, what *is* a good customer—and who decides? Never mind, you're supposed to bring in customers, and that's what you are measured against. Even worse, in this discipline of bringing in new customers, the count starts anew each month.

Moreover, you have to service customers, a task getting increasingly difficult as customers become more demanding and better informed—even if such information tends to be rather superficial and incomplete, which does not make things easier. Each customer brought in yesterday has to be serviced today and tomorrow.

A while ago you calculated the number of customers you could still bring in, provided you wanted to be able to spend enough time servicing each of them. You really had no choice, however, as monthly customer acquisition targets had to be met. Luckily, you were able to solve the riddle in your own way. Your solution had two parts:

1. You put in more work time.
2. You spent less time on each customer.

In that way you could continue to bring in new customers, meeting the targets you were being measured against, even though little or no time was left to service those same customers.

Let us come back to Smith, one of those customers you brought in years ago. Back then you promised him, "I'm always there for you. I'll service you on a regular basis. If in the meantime there is anything, just give me a call." Well, from time to time he actually does call, and so you, the stressed out acquirer and servicer of customers, are having regular feelings of guilt.

Smith has done quite a lot of business with you. He is certainly a good customer. When recently categorizing your customers, you gave him an A, the best possible mark. You can totally rely on him. However, can he also rely on you? Each year on the 22nd of December you drown your feelings of guilt in a bottle of red wine. Rather than having a private booze party, you take the red wine to Smith. Recently, though, you started to send it by post. That's much easier. Time has become so precious!

Smith has never campaigned for you. Nor did you ever ask. You would not even campaign for yourself, would you? It's really too bad!

You should finally try and sleep again. You'll have to get up early in the morning, at 6 o'clock when the alarm goes off. There is a handy post-it note pad on your bedside cabinet, on which you drowsily scribble "Smith".

As you doze off you have a final thought: *There must be another solution.*

ROTH AGAIN!

> The most things we learn, we learn from our customers.
> —Charles Lazarus

THE CLASS C CUSTOMER

382. There it is again. The display doesn't lie. Sooner or later, everyone gets familiar with the final three digits of this phone number. Even the apprentice—whom, I think, we introduced to them right in the second week.

Someone who calls in, again and again, once a month, or even more often? Usually he does so at 5.30 p.m. That is half an hour before office closing time—at least in theory. Today it is Barbara's turn to answer, as she has not had the pleasure for quite a while. Sometimes he even drops in. As soon as his head pops up in the window spirits drop. Some feel the spontaneous urge to visit the loo. A grim sense of humour takes over. Roth again!

Whether he phones in or stops by, the time requirement is enormous. He doesn't actually have any important questions, and he certainly doesn't generate significant sales. He has, however, a lot to tell you. What is special about Roth is that he has been there for years—or maybe even decades? In some distant past—it must have been in the last millennium—a mini customer relationship had been established. And he has been there ever since. He has never once brought in any more significant business! He wants to be serviced, asking questions nobody else is asking. He calls it customer service—and so do we. According to our company brochure, "We are always there for you, guaranteed". It goes without saying that we are there for Roth.

Most of the time he wants to talk to the boss, as he did back when the first contact was established. For the past two or three years, however, the boss has pretended that he's not there. Recently Roth asked whether our boss was still working with us, so we told him he is constantly on the road where he can't easily be reached. "He may as well pay me a visit. How about next week?" Roth replied. The boss was absolutely delighted, as you can imagine!

Sure, customers like Roth deserve to be taken care of. Actually, we have more of that sort; at least two-thirds of our customers may be of Roth's category, though none of them requires as much attention or poses as many questions as Roth. Roth is in early retirement, so he has time. We don't!

A year ago we tried to categorize our customers into class A, B, and C customers. Roth ended up in class C, with a tendency to D. But there was a problem. How to explain to a class C customer that he or she is a class C customer? Even more important, who will explain to a class C customer that he or she is a class C customer? What does servicing a class C customer look like? Our boss finally said, "Let's leave it as it is. Try to use up less time on class C customers—five or ten minutes should be enough." How can I do that? Am I to put up an hourglass and shoo the customer away as soon as the sand has run out?

Barbara bravely stands her ground, interjecting hardly any word herself—a sure sign of Roth being the person at the other end of the line—just "hmm" and "yes", alternately. Today Roth seems to be particularly communicative, as Barbara is saying even less than usual. The boss arrives, and a brief glance at the display puts him in the know. His vigorous shake of his head says: "I'm not here" —at least not for Roth.

It's just before 6 p.m. In a moment I'll call it a day. Barbara is still on duty …

I'M LEAVING

> Profits measure how well we serve customers.
> —Ken Melrose

A POTENTIAL CUSTOMER'S REPORT

For nearly two decades I have been Meyer's customer. Today, once again I was approached by one of his competitors. I actually liked what they said. They asked whether I was ready to switch. I would pay less and get more, they said. That's what they all say. Who is able to verify it? Additionally they offered me a service guarantee. Guaranteed availability, regular service contacts, and so on.

Well, that's exactly what Meyer promised back when we started to do business. It is probably part of a seller's vocabulary and not to be taken seriously. "I'm always there for you", he said congenially. That was the reason why we decided to work with him. Later, however, not much happened. Every Christmas we received a postcard with some hackneyed saying. The last two years it was the same card twice. They obviously reused what was left over from the previous year, thinking quite wrongly that no one would notice. Recently I read an ad of theirs, where they claimed to offer *service at its best*. I don't even want to imagine what the other forms of service would look like.

Is there anything I can do? Should I give them a call and beg for service? "They'll get in touch, if necessary", my wife says. Maybe she is right. But wouldn't it be better if they got in touch from time to time even without an urgent need, just to let us feel that they care?

Yesterday there was a television report on *service desert Germany*. Customer service has become the domain of machines instead of human beings, replacing more and more service staff. It could be so easy to stay in contact with customers. Is it because there are simply too many of them for a single staff member to take care of? In that case, please don't bother mentioning service in the first place. Anyhow, surely I shouldn't be expected to sympathise. My wife says, "You are expecting too much"; however, is it too much to expect from others to care a little bit for their customers?

I can't say that I'm satisfied. That's a pity, really, especially as our current account representative with Meyer is very nice. Also, our service needs have increased, so what should we do? Stay with Meyer or switch? The other company looked promising, with its modern look and feel, friendly staff, best availability and excellent prices. Whether I will still be happy there in two years' time remains to be seen, of course. Maybe their promises are just hot air too ...

Some time ago we changed our bank, for the same reasons—non-existent customer service, ever-increasing fees and unfriendly staff. It was quite stressful, with the paperwork and all. But in the end it was worth it, I swear!

We aren't the bargain-hunter type, willing to change business partners to save €3.70. We just want to be cared for a little bit, so that we can feel that we are doing the right thing. We aren't customers bent on getting the best service ever. We would even settle for a service that is just good.

That is to say, I've already made up my mind. I'm leaving.

2.

THE NON-SYSTEMATIC APPROACH TO WORKING WITH CUSTOMERS

GREEN FROGS IN A RED BUCKET

> Many are obstinate with regard to the once-chosen path, few with regard to the goal.
> —Friedrich Nietzsche

BACK TO THE BEGINNING

In Chapter 1 we saw some live reports from the selling front, each from a different perspective. Now, let's go back to the beginning: to the very start of a selling career. For both individual salespeople and companies, the commitment and the effort spent in acquiring new customers are enormous. Often, acquiring new customers is the only focus, as there isn't anything else to be done. Step by step, new customers are reached. Whether this happens in a strategic way—that is, based on a well-conceived business plan—is another question.

Imagine a big red bucket. Do you see it in your mind? Let all the customers gained by a salesperson be tiny green frogs. Can you imagine them? They will accompany us here and there in this book. What do you think a salesperson with a big red bucket and a new customer—aka frog—will do? Exactly, they'll put it into the bucket. There the frog is safe. Later our salesperson will gain more customers and put them into the bucket ... and still more ... and so on for weeks, months, and years. They all go into the bucket.

At the beginning, our salesperson still manages to care for his big bucket, with its not-too-many frogs. The salesperson can reach into the bucket, pick a frog and attend to it. He or she can see all the frogs happily sitting at the bottom of the bucket, and is able to care for each of them. The frogs also feel good. The salesperson manages to attend to them whilst gaining new frogs. Both tasks fit conveniently into the timetable.

As the years go by, the bucket gets fuller and fuller. The salesperson can't see all the frogs any more. Some of them they wouldn't even recognize, as frogs change over the years, not to mention the fact that those dwelling further down may feel quite uncomfortable.

From time to time, some frog manages to climb up the inside of the bucket and peek over the rim. In this case, the frog's need or wish gets the salesperson's attention, but it is hauled back into the bucket a moment later.

THE FEELING THAT THERE ARE UNCARED-FOR CUSTOMERS ...

How do you feel as the owner of a bucket full of uncared-for frogs? Sure, some of your frogs don't notice that they are not cared for, unless another seller passes by carrying an air-conditioned bucket with a relaxing wet zone, a patch of moisturizing moss and maybe a small shelter and some other amenities. If, additionally, the competition offers a favourable price-performance ratio for travelling in the bucket, regularly pays attention and builds a real relationship, your frogs sure will be tempted to switch buckets.

As a seller, your job is not just to gain customers. Sellers are there to care for their customers. The problem is, there comes a point where you aren't able to do so any more. So you need a care-taking plan—more about that later. Attending to your customers should be integral, part a plan that serves to strengthen and expand your customer relationships. To be able to do this even as your customer base is growing, you need a systematic approach. Today, developing standard practices is vital.

Establishing such practices is even more vital if you want to be able to delegate and outsource more and more of your care-taking tasks. Selling without a plan belongs to the past. I recommend that you keep a piece of paper handy—or your idea scratch pad if you have one—as you read the following pages and chapters. Jot down your thoughts and your ideas for implementing them. Most of our thoughts are quite ephemeral. Pin them down before you read on!

SALESPERSON GONE MEANS CUSTOMERS GONE

> To regret one's own experiences is to arrest one's
> own development.
> —Oscar Wilde

THE INCISIVE EVENT THAT LETS YOU ACT

Maybe your class A customer care process isn't unique and your feelings about your Smiths & Co. are less than satisfactory. Maybe your class C customer care process isn't clearly defined. Maybe you don't have a plan for the Roths of this world. There is certainly widespread need for improvement. Most people, however, hesitate to take the next step. They wait until they feel a certain degree of pain before they actually do something about their situation.

- What sort of pain would make you rethink your customer care process?
- What sort of pain would make you willing to systematize your way of working?

I'd like to tell you a little story. A salesperson for a financial services provider had managed to establish 1,300 customer relationships in fifteen years. He was getting some help from a co-worker who did some of the administrative work for about fifteen hours a week. Everything else, including the actual caring for the customers, the salesperson did himself. Some of his business contacts were hugely profitable while others were rather weak. He himself adhered to the principle of an absolute service, which was virtually the same for all customers. According to his solidarity-based sense of justice, each of his customers had put their trust in him. So he simply didn't want to let them down.

As his to-do list grew longer and longer, he responded by putting in more working time. First he stayed longer in the evenings, then he started earlier in the mornings and began to work on Saturdays. Finally he secretly worked even on Sundays. He gradually turned into a workaholic, deceiving himself that it was just a temporary peak in the workload. What all this meant for his private life I'm not going to describe here. Sometimes life is full of construction sites ...

For all his effort and commitment, however, he stood no chance of coping with the task. Quite the contrary, more and more customers complained about answers to their inquiries arriving too late. Customers with an interest in doing more business complained about offers not being sent out. Customers who were (or better: should have been) excellent VIP customers were being put off, as our salesperson didn't even have time for them. Whilat he put in maximum time and effort it was a task he simply couldn't cope with. His ambition and his quality service pledge— "I'll always be there for you" —gradually became an impossibility. And yet he stuck to it firmly.

When I met him, he was quite down. Notwithstanding this, he wasn't prepared to give up tasks, work more systematically, or expand his workforce. A short conversation on the occasion of one of my lectures had not been sufficient to convince him to rethink his approach. Let me repeat what I said at the beginning of this chapter. The time may not yet be right for change if the pain is not acute enough. Our salesperson thought he was doing the right thing, but he was in fact completely wrong.

One day about a year-and-a-half later, he called me. After listening for a minute or two, I remembered who he was—a challenge I sometimes struggle with, as so many people cross my path at a huge number of events. Some, however, do leave a mark, and he was one of them. He told me that he was finally willing to restructure his work. I was eager, of course, to learn the reason for this change of mind.

It was the pain! His office assistant of many years had left him, as she was tired of working in a disorganized chaos without having any areas of responsibility that were her own. Moreover, three of his best corporate customers had jointly left him, complaining that the quality of care had declined to an extent they were no longer prepared to put up with. These three customers alone accounted for about 8 percent of the total value of all his customers.

Neither of these losses were life-threatening for him, thank God. They provided, however, the necessary pain for him to take the next step. Today, out of his nearly 1,400 customers, there are 350 he himself attends to. Another 500 are cared for by an employed account manager, whilst the remaining 550 receive office services only. The whole arrangement has been skilfully communicated and professionally moulded into processes and procedures.

YOUR SITUATION MAY BE DIFFERENT, BUT ...

Your current situation may be quite different to the one described here. Nevertheless, your work can similarly be taken to the next quality level, for the benefit of yourself and your customers. You may not even need to expand your workforce. It may just be a matter of systemizing and simplifying your work.

It may be a matter of eliminating unimportant or outdated tasks or outsourcing routine activities. Ultimately, it is a question of how much time you have to spend on caring for customers, especially those who have a significant positive impact on your profits.

What sort of pain makes you act?

HELP! I AM STAGNATING

No case is lost unless you give up on it.
—Gottfried Ephraim Lessing

FIRST SUCCESSES DESTROY THE VERY ROOTS OF SUCCESS

The previous example was one of many. Often it is persistent selling that salespeople owe their first successes to. The business starts to run solidly. Successes become more frequent. The number of customers grows. It is, however, precisely these successes during the first years that stand in the way of continued selling success. As the administrative work and the various accompanying tasks increase, the time actually available for selling decreases. Which is a shame, really.

From my experience of counselling sellers in various industries, there are several reasons why successful careers may start to flag, leading to stagnation. On the following pages, I'll present the most common of these reasons, some of which you may be familiar with.

REASON FOR STAGNATION #1:
I KNOW BEST HOW TO DO THESE THINGS

In order to develop your work as a salesperson or a business owner, from time to time you have to make sure you spend your time and energy on tasks that are ever more specialized. As long as you do the same work today as you did yesterday you will earn the same profit today as you did yesterday. So during the first years of your development, if you don't get rid of one task or another, you won't be able to devote yourself to more profitable tasks. By sticking to the kind of work a clerk is supposed to do you will continue to be paid like a clerk.

Now you may (rightly) say: "I know best how to do this." It would certainly be a poor lookout if you didn't. After all, you are the most experienced person in this area of work. By performing less profitable tasks, however, you prevent yourself from taking on more profitable ones. In order to keep developing, you have to increase the value of what you do in accordance with your increased experience. Otherwise, that experience is wasted—a pity, as well as a financial loss.

The design of your developmental process depends on you. You may adopt a new strategic orientation and get rid of certain less profitable tasks or customers. You may also get other people on board who are less expensive than yourself to take over certain tasks. Of course, it will take some time before they are up to your quality standards. You will have to provide them with room for development and empowerment, as well as clear directives.

For outsourcing to function well, you must state in clear terms what you want. Ideally, jot down, in a few words, how you expect a certain task to be implemented. By doing so you avoid misunderstandings and lay the groundwork for consistent quality and execution—in your company's or your own personal hue. (There is more to come about how to describe these tasks so that they are executed in a consistent fashion.)

Hand over tasks boldly. Learn from your experiences. Not everything will go smoothly. Not every handover will live up to your expectations. You will not be able to easily get rid of every task. Some will keep coming back like boomerangs, as you have been the one who knew best so far. This doesn't mean, however, that you are on the wrong path. These are just the teething troubles of your next developmental stage, your next quality level. Corporate development is a learning process.

Another reason for stagnation is the lack of desire for change and development and the time needed to indulge in it. Some people simply don't have it or don't make it ...

REASON FOR STAGNATION #2:
I NEITHER HAVE TIME FOR NOR DESIRE CHANGE

The second reason that companies stagnate is even more critical: familiar, *proven* routine versus necessary change. Your work processes, task allocation and customer care procedures have stood the test of time. Processes can't be changed over night. Moreover, it would cost more time than leaving everything as it is. The growth of the business comes with so many tasks that it's nearly impossible to cope with all of them—not to mention find the time and energy needed to change things.

Organizations tend to be the same. As a rule, people are so entrenched in their routines that change appears too time-consuming. In some cases, however, the whole organizational chart has to be restructured. Who should be responsible for what? Who will attend to which customer? Exactly how should production and sales work together? Which tasks can be systemized in which ways?

Who is supposed to do all of that? Since these changes require a huge effort above and beyond normal operations, they must be a daily point of focus. Someone has to be in charge of them. It is not enough for a business owner or a salesperson to take a day off from time to time, in order to focus on company development or how things should be changed. Improving how you do business must be a top priority, ongoing selling operations notwithstanding. Your high-speed train needs to be repaired whilst travelling at full speed.

For all this to happen, there needs to be someone who is aware of how important developmental processes are and who takes the time to deal with them. Otherwise you may be in for a vicious cycle. Being completely stressed out, you cannot find the time to change your approach. Your stress level increases, leaving you with even less time. Your desire to deal with development steadily decreases.

Seen from the outside, organizational charts and task allocation quickly become outmoded and inappropriate as cues for the next developmental steps. What are needed are new priorities, new task allocation patterns and possibly individual development processes. A business consultancy can be of help, especially for planning the details. Sustainable implementation, however, requires consistent action on your part after the initial consultation has taken place.

REASON FOR STAGNATION #3:
I CAN'T AFFORD TO INVEST

Common reasons for stagnation include lack of time or lack of desire for change. Some business owners or salespeople would like to change but can't. Many are willing to take the next developmental step, invest in people, establish new procedures and enter the next growth stage. Financial resources, however, do not allow it.

If this is your situation, a quick analysis will reveal that your calculations up to this point have not been coherent. Your earnings haven't matched your operating costs and other expenses, leaving you with no net profit. Maybe your personal withdrawals have been higher than justified by your profits. Perhaps your earnings were too low compared to your expenses. One reason for low earnings could be a less than adequate frequency of customer contacts. If, however, your appointment quota has been excellent, there are still two possible reasons. You may have talked to the wrong customers—strategically speaking—or there may be weaknesses in your sales process. Or your product or service may not be marketable.

If you simply lack the financial means to take the next developmental step, you should take a critical look in the rear-view mirror. Why is your return so low? What things can you change? Be aware that your inability to invest makes the actual quality of your success so far rather questionable. From an operational point of view you may have been successful, but from a strategic perspective your performance has not been sufficient.

I suggest, therefore, that you establish a business plan which includes your calculated expenses for development as soon as possible. You will then be able to align your processes with your business plan. In addition, build up a return that will enable you to finance further development.

REASON FOR STAGNATION #4:
MY CUSTOMERS EXPECT INDIVIDUAL SOLUTIONS

You may rightly ask whether trust-based customer relationships would still be possible if you didn't attend to your customers individually. It might be possible in some industries, but certainly not in yours, you may think. After all, what customers want is to be cared for individually ...

You are right, of course. It's all about trust and individuality. At the same time, however, you are digging a grave for your dreams of future growth because soon you will be unable to cope. More and more things will have to wait for you to individually attend to them. More and more customers won't be cared for at all, as you won't be able to keep up with all of them individually. Individuality demands more and more of your time as a salesperson. You increasingly get a bad conscience for not managing to do everything according to your quality standards. An agonizing quest for perfection becomes the very source of stagnation.

As your business grows, at some point you will need systems and standard practices that make your life of operations and sales easier. You need automated procedures in order to be certain that even as customer numbers increase you are still able to do what you have always wanted to do—that is, to combine excellent sales activities with outstanding customer service. The more you grow, the more you will be able to delegate jobs based on clear standards. If you were to keep growing while sticking to your previous notion of individuality you would be left with the single option of cloning yourself.

Not being able to provide individual service as you used to do when your customers could still be counted in dozens is the price of growth. Using first class procedures, however, you will still be able to provide quality sales and services far superior to those the individual business owner or salesperson who hates standard practices and refuses to delegate can offer.

I therefore suggest that you use excellent, well-crafted procedures to ensure that your customer service processes are top-quality. The outcome can be much more rewarding and valuable for your customers than anything you offered them before.

REASON FOR STAGNATION #5:
MY CUSTOMERS WANT TO BE ATTENDED TO BY ME, NOT SOMEBODY ELSE

Business owners and salespeople frequently tell me that their customers want to be attended to by them only. Development is well and good, they say, but firstly, you have to find the right people, and secondly, it requires your customers to accept being attended to by somebody else, be it field staff instead of the business owner or office staff instead of the salesperson they are familiar with.

Let's start with the customer who wants to be attended to by no one else but you. You would certainly have cause to worry if this were not the case. After all, isn't this trust the very reason why that person became your customer in the first place? Why should they want to be attended to by someone else, someone with whom they can't be sure what to expect? And to be honest, who doesn't feel flattered by such unconditional trust?

For business owners, however, true entrepreneurial quality starts when your customers don't just trust you personally, but the whole environment you have built up around you, in other words, when you move from being a business to having a business where quality customer care exists independently of you.

If you are a salesperson, the more tasks you are able to delegate, the more you are free to do the thing you are (hopefully) especially good at—the thing that actually appears on your business card.

For that to happen, of course, you need clear processes and procedures that can be realized by others, and staff or partners that are at the same level of quality. The clearer these procedures and the more promising your sales and service concept, the sooner you will be able to find the right people to assist you. Professional organizing capabilities are often a magnet for outstanding people—who, in turn, frequently lack this very talent.

REASON FOR STAGNATION #6:
I DON'T WANT TO WORK EVEN MORE

Your development during recent years and your growing number of customers have made your job ever more challenging and time-consuming. Sooner or later a point is reached where you simply can't put in more working time. If your business grows any further you will be left with no private life at all. That is too high a price ...

As far as looking in the rear-view mirror goes, this assessment is correct. What has happened so far is closely related to the issues mentioned above. You have done everything yourself—in a very individual fashion and often without an adequate systematic approach. If further development of your business would lead to your twelve-hour working day permanently becoming a fourteen-hour and then a sixteen-hour working day, doubts are in order, as this certainly wouldn't look like healthy development. The growth of your business would be coming at the expense of your private life. No wonder you have started to lose interest in growing any further.

This is why I insist that you systemize your tasks and procedures in order to be able to increasingly delegate them in a professional way. That's how sustainable development works, for business owners as well as for salespeople. Most importantly, that's how to avoid development coming at the expense of your health.

It is a myth that your working time inevitably increases in proportion to the growth of your business. If that is the case it simply shows that you need to organize your activities much more professionally. Building a professional organization will be your next challenge!

REASON FOR STAGNATION #7:
I'M NOT SURE HOW THINGS WILL CHANGE AROUND ME

Recent years have certainly brought about a lot of changes in the way you do business: new laws and regulations, technological innovations, changes in customer demographics, and new marketing approaches for your products and services. Since you don't know what changes may be coming next, you hesitate to initiate changes yourself. Instead, you wait to see if and how the market will further evolve.

In recent years, significant changes have taken place, including technological innovations and the acceleration of your own work. The pace of change will not slow down any time soon. On the contrary, nobody knows what the selling environment will look like in 2020, not to mention 2030. What we do know for sure, however, is that there will still be a need for tailor-made products and services based on each customer's needs and wishes.

As complexity increases it will be more and more difficult to keep sight of the whole picture. Forms of communication such as social media will continue to change and evolve. Customer expectations will increase. Businesses that are well-positioned will be able to benefit from the opportunities provided by the market. What about you?

For business owners as well as salespeople, it is essential to vigilantly investigate the potential risks and opportunities brought by any current changes. The more professionally you are positioned and the more selling power you command, the better you can take advantage of the various opportunities as they present themselves. Waiting for certainty regarding change is not an appropriate entrepreneurial sales approach. Instead, think of a car: it can only be steered whilst in motion.

I suggest, therefore, that you adopt a positive attitude and look for opportunities to build a solid future for your business. Develop professional processes and procedures that enable you to take advantage of your talents and possibilities. This will benefit your customers, your potential staff and, last but not least, yourself.

THE END OF THE CONDITIONAL

> Some of us think holding on makes us strong
> but sometimes it is letting go.
> —Hermann Hesse

WHAT IS THE CAUSE OF YOUR STAGNATION?

In the previous section I described the seven main causes of stagnation. Which of these might be the cause of your own stagnation? In lectures and seminars and when working with clients I often hear sentences like these:

- "We should revise our procedures."
- "We might do something for our class A customers."
- "We should revise our consulting approach."
- "We could refresh our homepage."
- "We should put our heads together."

None of these conditional statements represents an entrepreneurial attitude. If there is anything you should, could or might do, why don't you just do it? Philosophizing vaguely about what has to be done doesn't befit a business owner or a salesperson committed to growing their business and engaging in active selling. It is even less appropriate for a business owner or a salesperson to dodge responsibility by hiding behind a collective *we*.

As much as it may appear to be against the team spirit and the imperative to work together, it is your job to define developmental priorities. You are the head of the business, so you have to take the lead—whilst encouraging others to join in, of course.

If, in the past, you did not succeed in realizing a project it was ultimately because you didn't deem it important enough. Now you will think, *if only you knew how much I had on my plate ...* So which tasks can you get off that plate? On whose plate could you put them? What should your procedures look like so that you are able to pay those who take them over? In which ways are you able to automate tasks?

It is your job to work hard on this one. It is your job to redefine your role in existing projects in such a way that there is room for you to once again act as an entrepreneur. I will not say it is easy. The easiest thing for you to do is certainly to take care of all the things on your desktop yourself. But that wouldn't be smart: there are alternatives that are significantly cheaper, provided you are capable of and committed to using the time freed up in such a way that the additional revenues generated are higher than the expenses for delegating the tasks. Are you confident that you are able to do that?

PERFECTION BEATS ENTREPRENEURSHIP

It is exactly this self-confidence that is one of the most important features of any business owner or salesperson committed to investment and growth. Be careful, however! Some people may be so sure of themselves—their intelligence, their abilities, their impact on customers, and their being perfect—that there isn't the slightest chance for anyone else to match their quality standards.

As a result, they fall back into doing too many things themselves. These people may be self-employed, but in their minds they aren't entrepreneurs. Their desire for perfection gets the better of their sense of entrepreneurship. That's too bad, as they will probably always have to content themselves with *we should ...* and *I should ....*

I would like to encourage the rest of you who are eager to take the route of entrepreneurial development to work on what you are doing and to fine-tune your processes. Business owners and salespeople committed to growing their business and engaging in active selling know how to step back from time to time to observe themselves. They constantly work on becoming better and more effective.

Now is your chance to usher in the end of the conditional! Next, let's get to grips with the systematic approach to working with customers.

3.

A SYSTEMATIC APPROACH TO WORKING WITH CUSTOMERS

PART A — THE PRECONDITIONS

THE SECRET: A SYSTEMATIC APPROACH

> Anyone who has never made a mistake has never tried anything new.
> —Attributed, among others, to Albert Einstein

IF BEING TRULY "INDIVIDUAL" ISN'T AN OPTION ANY MORE

Sales routine is characterized by a multitude of business events. Customers send inquiries via traditional mail, fax, e-mail, text, or social media. They appear on your doorstep, or you knock on their doors. There are many routes leading from the customer to you—or from you to the customer, for that matter. If you already have "a number of customers", you must take care that you still have time left to "do sales".

Today, you have to procure your bits of information from various sources and contact your customers in a multitude of ways. Which sources and what means you use is up to you—or to your competitors, whom you certainly shouldn't ignore. The way today's customers will contact you is similarly varied.

It is easy to see that it becomes more and more difficult to juggle all of this, and even more so if you are committed to adhering to a maximum level of individuality in what you do. The problem is that the way you intuitively react to various events, questions, and situations is unique and inimitable. You simply can't clone yourself. The more customers you have, the more difficult it becomes for you to maintain your own service and quality status quo.

Sooner or later you will need to adopt a consistent way of reacting to these events, questions and situations. To start with you may get away with less, but even then a response makes things a lot easier. For this, you need standard practices. Such practices reduce the time needed for thinking and enable activity patterns to be copied.

Of course, this also means a loss of individuality, but then again I know a lot of businesses where the owner, for all his high quality standards, becomes increasingly unreliable—because issues are being put off until he himself gets round to them. Finally attending to them with the usual— albeit slightly rushed—individuality does not compensate for the delay. He simply can't keep up anymore.

Here, if not before, standard practices come into play. But what exactly are standard practices?

Such practices may include:

- checklists to be ticked off
- consulting agendas and folders
- phone call guidelines for various occasions
- face-to-face guidelines for various occasions
- courses of action for various customer classes
- courses of action for personnel management
- etc.

Each of these practices defines a corridor of action for your business. By defining these practices you standardize your special way of acting. You put into written form your intuitive way of dealing with your customers and of performing your daily business, thereby making sure that you and each of your employees follows your pattern. After all, you know how you think, how you act, and how you proceed.

RELEASE YOUR PARKING BRAKE!

A standard definition doesn't cover all possible situations, but it does at least cover most of them. To the stressed-out business owner or salesperson who has been doing most of the work himself or herself I would say: you will be freed from many of the burdens that have hitherto been your exclusive "privilege".

Of course, there is no secret involved. This chapter's title has it wrong. The fact is, even though such a small number of business owners and salespeople perform in a professional way, these few are achieving outstanding success. One might be induced to think that standard practices must indeed have some mystique about them, but it is not so. Most people would stick to their personal individuality rather than resolve to release their parking brake.

WHO EXACTLY IS YOUR CUSTOMER?

> Ignoranti quem portum petat nullus suus ventus
> est. (For those who don't know to which port they
> are sailing, no wind is right.)
> —Seneca the Younger

THE VERY BEGINNING OF ESTABLISHING STANDARD PRACTICES

Who exactly is your customer? "What a question", you might think. "Isn't my customer whoever benefits from the work I do? It's these very customers, after all, that my business is all about." Unfortunately, though, "customer" is quite a vague term.

In order to be able to understand this better, let us imagine starting, for example, a gym. You may decide that all inhabitants of the region are potential customers—quite conceivable, especially if yours is the only gym operating in the neighbourhood. Maybe you don't even need to advertise too aggressively in order for customers to come and seek you out. After all, customers looking for a gym are left with no alternative. The only thing they need to be informed about is that you exist. Of course, it is seldom as easy as that.

Since the absence of competition makes business a lot easier, you may be tempted to treat its challenges more lightly. And so you tend to make less effort and do business rather perfunctorily and with less care, since you are sure that your customers will come back to you anyway.

This situation changes as soon as others become aware of your "gold mine" and open a second gym not far from yours. Well, competition certainly breathes life into business and turns a market upside down. Some customers drift away while others stay. Now, you have the task of considering possible reasons for your customers to stay with your "gym". The better you have defined who you want to be your customer, the easier this step will be.

If you are targeting the fitness-seeking population under 25, for instance, your external impact, interior design, and choice of background music should be different from what would be appropriate for the young-at-hearts. You may need different equipment, as your target group will be concerned with abdominal muscles rather than back muscles, or with visual effects rather than knee problems.

The kind of additional offers your customers would appreciate also depends on your target group. The more customers with their specific needs and wishes are able to identify with you, the more likely they will come back and recommend you to their group, thus becoming your free-of-charge advertising media. Even your fitness coaches may vary depending on your customer profile. Think about it.

FOR WHOM DO YOU CREATE STANDARD PRACTICES AND PROCEDURES?

In order to be able to make the right decisions and establish the right process and care systems, you have to identify your specific target group. Here are some questions you may ask:

- Who exactly is your customer?
- Where and how do you "find" your customer?
- Are there multipliers in this—your—group of customers?

Let's come back to your business and selling activities. Self-employed people often tend to spend huge sums on marketing to get the attention of various people, most of whom never become their customers. Whilst such an approach may be interesting for big companies, small and middle-sized businesses with a limited geographic scope are well advised to use a more targeted approach, and not only for budget reasons.

The driving factor for such a wide marketing approach is the desire for fame rather than any economic rationale. You may have heard of so-called "hidden champions" —businesses that, often unbeknownst to the crowds, act as regional or even global market leaders in their own little niche, such as Stabilo and Webasto, to name just two. Did you know they existed? Even if you didn't, it hasn't done those businesses any harm. Whether everybody knows about them or not is of secondary importance since it has no impact on their business success.

For a number of reasons, it is essential to know your customer base. Only by knowing who they are and what they need will you be able to fulfil 100 percent of their requirements—or, in the ideal case, even more than that.

So who is your customer? Think about this carefully.

DO YOU PROVIDE THE RIGHT CUSTOMERS WITH THE RIGHT SERVICE?

> The biggest decision in your life is that you can change your life by changing your attitude.
> —Albert Schweitzer

SMITH AND CO.

A prerequisite for successful sales is to be close to your customers, interested in your customers and successful with your customers. More than that—you have to be close to the right customers, interested in the right customers and successful with the right customers. Not surprisingly, I call the right customers class A customers. Incidentally, one among them was Smith. Do you remember him? Having scrutinized your customers you may now ask who among them are your "right" customers—your potential class A customers?

Many companies and many salespeople are proud of their huge customer base—1,000 customers, 2,000 customers, 5,000 customers. For them a customer is a person who once bought something from them. Ever since, this person has been part of their customer base. There they stay until for whatever reason they get in touch again via e-mail, phone, or in person because they have another need. In the meantime, they get selected from time to time to receive a letter or an e-mail—just in case ...

Fundamental to every business and every sales activity is the question: Which customers do you really want to reach? Which customer do you want to do "business" with? Without an answer to this question, you can't do business in a professional way and sell successfully. Instead, what you get is random sales and random growth. Then, you will often hear, "I take what I get ..."

Businesses who cannot target their customers aren't able to attend to them appropriately, because they don't know them. Don't allow your customers to get lost in your customer base. You need a plan to care for the "right" customers in the "right" way. Everything else is just average and will not stand out. As soon as your neglected customer runs into someone who offers truly systematic customer care, they will be gone, just like what happened in the gym example above. Once again:

1. Think about who your "right" customer is. Be as specific as possible.
2. Plan exactly how you are going to care for these "right" customers.

You cannot implement a truly consistent customer care concept if you don't even know who you have developed it for. Moreover, it goes without saying that the right customers should let you earn money, possibly even big profitable money so that you are able to reinvest in your business and develop it.

Even then, of course, you will have customers who don't fit the model; however, they are still your customers, even though they don't belong to your target group. Caring for them will be easier now, and will not take up as much time and energy as before. As a rule, these customers are less profitable, since they have applied for a less comprehensive or a different type of customer care.

You won't be able to transform your customers into true fans of your customer care process until you know how to describe them, so that you can really benefit from them. My blog www.ritterblog.de would not have so many frequent visits if it wasn't clearly focused on my target group. Our institute wouldn't grow year by year if we hadn't clearly defined our target customers. Focus ensures growth. Even if you know it like no other, you cannot become your market's #1 until you have defined it.

PREPARATION: CLASS A, CLASS B, AND CLASS C CUSTOMERS

> "What can I do", says Zeus.
> —Friedrich Schiller

CUSTOMER GROUPS: FAIR OR NOT?

You are now clear on who should be your customer. So far, so good. The next point of focus is to understand that as soon as the number of customers who need care exceeds your ability to care for them, they will begin to divide into "wheat" and "chaff". Even if a salesperson doesn't classify and label their customers deliberately, they will do it intuitively in the course of their daily routine. They will therefore attend to some customers whilst letting others fall through the cracks.

The most important customers are generally those who are more profitable and have more potential than others. They may also be customers who play a multiplier role. Less important customers include those who are less profitable and have less potential for development. However, does this warrant a classification of customers into classes A, B, and C, or maybe even Z?

You might argue that such a class is neither service-oriented nor just. After all, each customer deserves to receive the best possible care. On the other hand, a business must be economically viable. If a customer wishes or expects a service exceeding the budget, then there is something wrong with the business concept. A situation in which a customer yields insufficient profit must be avoided. Either they aren't fit to be a customer in the first place, or by placing a small order they purchase just a small service package. This must be clearly defined in the business concept, as well as clearly communicated.

Ultimately, this means that each customer relationship must be profitable to the company. It must at least generate an income that covers the expenses; otherwise the bottom line is negative and has to be subsidized by other customer relationships that are more profitable. This might be an option in some cases, but it has its limits.

For example, it is certainly not a good idea for a company to focus on customers who don't yield much profit—or even produce losses—as that means you will lack the time and resources to care for your best and most important customers.

If you are according the same amount of care to each customer, then your profitable customers should be entitled to send an end-of-year bill to your less profitable customers for a service paid for by the former and enjoyed by the latter.

It is therefore quite "fair" (if we may use such a word here) to provide certain customers with a so-called "basic support" that can be very streamlined and doesn't necessarily include your personal involvement as a salesperson. It may even be restricted to office-based support. Alternatively, provide to those customers who trust you completely, allowing you to earn a real profit, exclusive care with a truly commendable service package.

It is fair enough to care for your customers in different ways. Treating everybody in the same manner may sound good, but it bears no relation to economics. Using classes A, B, and C, or however you prefer to classify your customers, enables you to focus on those customers who help to secure your people's jobs and make your business viable. They are the ones, after all, who are committed to closely cooperating with you.

ASSESSING CUSTOMERS IN "COLD MONEY"?

The classification of customers as a necessary measure has its detractors as well as its proponents. One critical Twitter message addressed to me recently said, "My mantra is, treat each customer as if they were your only one. If you assess customers in cold money you are lost."

This view is widely shared. Classifying customers is perceived as cold and calculating, and as contradicting the very principles of service. The lower-ranking customer gets no more service and has to be disposed of. Recent attempts in the banking sector have not yet been forgotten. Of course, that's not exactly what I mean.

A class C customer should still get his service. This service, however, should be streamlined and based as far as possible on standard practices. After all, why should a class C customer who decided against a more comprehensive cooperation with you be entitled to receive services indefinitely and free of charge, just because he is "in some way" your customer?

As long as you don't take a decision about which customers will receive which services, there will be many unprofitable customers. You will not be able to care for those few customers who do yield a profit because you spend all of your time with those who do not. It has nothing to do with "cold money". It is all about the quality paid for by the customer. Let me repeat, class C customers receive service also, and this may be the industry standard and comparable to the service provided by potential competitors.

For those who have decided to cooperate with you more comprehensively you may provide an exclusive package. If this package is really appealing, they will recommend you to others. *Who* is recommending you is very important. Customers generally follow classes.

If a class A customer recommends you to another potential customer, you can safely assume that the latter isn't a class C customer. If you treat everybody the same, you would offer average service to all customers, as you wouldn't have the time and the financial means for more. This is only possible as long as the number of your customers remains small; as soon as you have more customers than you are able to care for based on the principle of equal treatment you have to make a decision.

If you have worked alone up to now, you are, of course, in a difficult position. How can you treat a class C customer differently from a class A customer? Well, there are options available. For example, some very successful sellers use the following scheme. (Please use it as a general guideline—don't stick to the details, as I am sure your situation is different. Use it as a source of inspiration for your future approach.)

Class A customers	Class C customers
On-site consultations	In-office consultations
Call-back on the same day	Call-back on the next day
Pro-active contacts on events	Reactive service only
Guaranteed annual checks	Checks on demand only
Invitations for customer events	No invitations
Quarterly printed newsletter	No newsletter or via e-mail only

As you can see, class C customers do get their service. However, service is not granted indiscriminately. If you treat each customer as if they were your one and only customer, it may well be that for that very reason you cannot get hold of more of your "right" customers.

A less profit-oriented approach to customer care may indeed be appealing to customers. It would certainly make you stand out from competitors who aren't able or prepared to commit to such a strategy. Sooner or later, however, you too will run out of puff, even if you work ten hours a day instead of eight, which will soon become twelve and more. Then you will have to decide.

By the way, I am writing this chapter sitting on an Austrian Airlines flight from Vienna via Dresden to Leipzig. Business class in the front and economy class in the back, with passengers allotted to one or the other on behalf of "cold money". However, no-one who sits in the back complains about not being served a newspaper. Obviously things have been clearly communicated beforehand ...

PART B — LEAD GENERATION AND CUSTOMER ACQUISITION

HOW SYSTEMATICALLY DO OTHERS BECOME AWARE OF YOU?

> Good work alone is not enough. You have to find someone who appreciates it.
> —Marcel Mart

THE END OF THE UNDERCOVER AGENT

Business owners and salespeople have to maintain a constant balancing act between existing and new customers. So before we talk about how you work with existing customers, I would like to focus on systematic lead generation and the customer acquisition process.

Arousing potential customers' curiosity is the first step of an effective customer acquisition process. At this point many salespeople ask themselves how they can improve their results—from a situation of effectively working "under cover". Being known to potential customers in a positive sense often makes for an advantage in terms of trust compared to others whom nobody has heard of. So be sure that your target customers become aware of you on a regular basis. This can be done in different—preferably systematic—ways. Out of the following examples, focus on those that are likely to help you reach your specific group of target customers. To use the frog metaphor, you have to know your frogs very well to be able to catch their attention.

TEN WAYS TO MAKE YOURSELF KNOWN

- Create small-scale or large-scale events to receive press coverage
- Do something for your community or your target group to draw media attention
- Get featured in a newspaper
- Write an interesting column for a newspaper
- Launch an award for your target group
- Publish a magazine for your community or your target group
- Launch a blog for your community or your target group
- Deliver attention-grabbing presentations at meetings
- Include regional and national celebrities
- Use crazy actions to spice up your image

For maximum impact you should do what you do on a regular basis. Welcome back to the fundamental idea of this book! Everything you do should take place automatically. That is what a "systematic approach to selling" is all about. Whatever you do just once has essentially no impact at all.

One-time action does not produce a lasting impact that sticks with the customer. It must happen for a second, third or n^{th} time before there is a change in the customer's perception. Only if something is repeated several times does the customer's mind associate you and your business with attributes such as "consistency" and "reliability". That is when you start to establish your place. Even if the customer doesn't yet know you confidence builds up. Each time you grab your customer's attention in a positive way, you stand out more clearly from your competitors.

The aim is therefore to make the process of "getting known" and "drawing attention" a systematic part of your way of doing business. If you can do something in this direction every month, every week or maybe even every day, or have others do it for you, you are certainly on the right track.

Establishing routine processes is priceless. No matter which route or routes you choose to take, don't hesitate to involve others in your activities. There is no need for you to do it all yourself, especially if others are better at it. Let me repeat: make sure to focus on actions that help you reach the right people. Only then will what you do really make sense.

Incidentally, I practice myself some of the above suggestions. Take, for instance, our magazine "Unternehmer-Ass" launched in 1999, the award "Unternehmer-Ass des Jahres" established in 2005, or the "Ritterblog" that went online in 2008. Each month I write several columns for the magazines read by my target groups. Not to mention Xing, Facebook, Twitter, etc...

HOW SYSTEMATICALLY DO OTHERS CAMPAIGN FOR YOU?

> Our customers are our best campaigners.
> —Rainer Megerle

DO YOU MAINTAIN COMPLEMENTARY PARTNERSHIPS?

Many businesses maintain complementary partnerships in which the partners recommend each other to their customers. Who do you recommend? Who recommends you?

You have probably seen on of these before:

- You go to the baker's, buy a loaf of bread, and are offered a one-dollar voucher for the butcher next door, or vice versa.
- You sit on a plane and are offered a discount on a recommended language course, or you visit a language course and receive a voucher for a free-of-charge snack with an airline.
- Beside your controlling report, your tax consultant sends you a recommendation for an attorney he is maintaining a partnership with, or vice versa.

Who could you recommend on a regular basis? Who could recommend you on a regular basis? For your inspiration, here are some examples from small and middle-sized businesses I have worked with.

- A local bookstore puts a card for customers to order a free-of-charge guidebook for your industry from your business in each paper bag. Likewise, on the last page of each of your brochures, you recommend three topic-related books available at "your" bookstore.

- A famous restaurant uses beer coasters advertising your business, each of them designed in an inspirational way using some motto like "did you know that ..." rather than just announcing your address and phone number. In return, each month you hold a draw for the birthday children among your "exclusive" customers to receive a 60-dollar voucher for visiting said restaurant.
- A tax consultant and you jointly publish a quarterly newsletter for each one's best 500 clients/customers, in which each of you prepare two pages featuring tax tips and tips for your industry, respectively.

INSPIRATION RATHER THAN BLUEPRINT

As before, these example aren't necessarily applicable one-to-one to your industry. Use them as a source of inspiration to develop your own ideas. Brainstorm together with your team. Look out for a complementary partner—or even two or three. Chances are that you'll find them among your customers. During such an event you can use your partnerships to attract new customers—or, better still, you can win new customers together. The motto is: "first provide value, then build trust." That way, customer relationships will just happen ...

HOW SYSTEMATICALLY DO YOU CONVERT POTENTIALS INTO CUSTOMERS?

> Love is three quarters curiosity.
> —Giacomo Girolamo Casanova

ENGAGING YOUR POTENTIAL CUSTOMERS

To begin with a quote by Casanova, how do we make sure that curiosity turns into true love? How can we transform an initial interest into a lasting relationship?

Over the years, each salesperson accumulates a number of potential customers. These are people who have once shown some form of interest in what we offer, without resolving to actually start a business relationship—for various different reasons.

So, what can we do? To begin with, there is a heap of data waiting to be put to proper use. Go for the systematic approach. Make sure that your potential customers hear from you, whether they ask to or not. That is not to say that you should constantly call them and ask whether they finally decided to place an order. Instead, take the initiative and offer something of value up front. Give first and take later.

Offer your potential customers value on a regular basis. Provide useful information that lets your business stand out. Keep your potential customers up to date about your field of activity. Make them aware of just how exciting you will be as a partner once they become your customer.

MAKE USE OF SO-CALLED AUTO-RESPONDERS

Technically this can be realized by way of, for instance, an auto-responder software that automatically provides potential customers with valuable or interesting information as soon as they contact you.

You write the e-mails once. Your potential customers then receive e-mails 1, 2, 3, etc. whenever a certain amount of time has lapsed since their last download. You may add more e-mails to make sure your inspirational input is always up-to-date. Make sure, however, not to press your potential customers too hard by asking them to "buy me" and "call me."

Apart from carefully nudging them into becoming your customer, you should leave it to them to decide when they are ready to place an order. Present practical examples, make suggestions based on your experiences, and provide real value. Keep the information clear, friendly and competent.

I frequently write on www.ritterblog.de along precisely these lines—my motto is "give first, take later". This is exciting, and requires me to think carefully and to see the world from the customer's perspective. As Ovid put it: "Giving is a work of true genius." There is an old Italian proverb: "Giving is fishing." So go fishing!

THE OLD REAL LIFE

Besides automated e-mail sending there is, of course, still the old analogue world. Besides the digital life, there is still real life—whatever that is ...

The digital world moves pretty quickly—click and go! It is difficult to catch customers' attention for more than a moment as they zap through browser tabs and social media channels. I suggest therefore that you continue to keep the erstwhile, the conservative, the apparently "old-fashioned" in mind.

The more people write text messages and post status messages, the more powerful an impact the old-fashioned postcard creates. Did I mention facsimiles? Most of the time, both will end up in the snail mail inbox where they may attract some real attention.

It is, of course, possible to digitally and automatically boost your potential customer database as has been described above. I suggest, however, that you go one step further. Make a list, hand-written or digital, containing all potential customers you are itching to turn into real customers. Put the list on your pin board or desk. Make sure it's always before your eyes.

Now make it your habit to regularly provide each of them with some personal value, give them a boost and help them feel good. This is not about promoting your products. It is about making these people feel how valuable it is to work with you before they even do. I am aware of the fact that such an approach doesn't qualify as "hardcore selling". Nevertheless it is effective—and sustainably so.

PROVIDING VALUE AND A GOOD FEELING

You may give a boost to everyone on your list, or just to one of them. Make a note, hand-written if you like, of the date and what it is that you will provide—to make sure that sooner or later it's everybody's turn. Repeat from time to time. Now you may think, "How long do I have to do this? When should I see results?" Well, this is certainly an investment, primarily an investment of time. Don't expect to see a slew of new customers in a matter of weeks, just go on.

Here are some examples of what you can do:

- Each time you read an interesting article, cut it out (or print it if it's online) and send it to a customer to whom this information may be of particular interest. On a yellow Post-It note or your business sticker add a line like "Thought this might interest you, best wishes, ..."
- You have a business partner who is interested in something that one of your potential customers has to offer. Send a note of recommendation to your business partner, make a copy, scribble "FYI, ..." on it and fax it to your potential customer.
- There is a positive newspaper report about one of your potential customers. Make a copy, write "Good job! ..." on it and fax it to the firm.

These three examples are just to illustrate what I mean. You can easily expand the list. It is important that you offer value with no strings attached. Make sure it feels good to the other person. For them, it will be a relief from daily stress. But don't do it with an attitude of "tomorrow

I will ask him when we will work together." Don't expect a favour in return. You will get it, as long as you don't expect to. Do a good job and don't give up.

Unlike your e-mail booster, here we have something tangible. Your handwriting adds to its personal character, signalling that you have taken time for it, a rarity today. It is a systematic approach to ensure that you look at the value equation from your customers' point of view, regularly giving them boosts, as documented by your list. Such an elaborate approach admittedly makes sense only for potential customers that are of great interest to you. You are not in the business of altruism, after all. By the way, you don't need to do everything yourself, provided you have someone to do it for you.

LEVERAGING FACEBOOK & CO.

Follow me once again from the real world to the digital. The world keeps turning, and the social media wave rolls on. In spite of all changes, the chances for businesses are enormous. Customers are open for dialogue, personal feedback is within reach, and there is maximum transparency.

Chances come with risks, of course. With the advent of web 2.0, you are no longer the only one who decides what is written about you and your business. Your customers join in the conversation, and they do it publicly. Search engines make their contributions accessible for all to read.

Certainly you can try and build a wall around your business—an approach ominously reminding me of the former GDR. The alternative is to face up to the world as it is, accept the freedom of speech that exists on the Internet and elsewhere, and simply join in. The best way to do that is to in take part in Facebook, Xing, Twitter, and Co.

Identify the media which are projected to attract the most rapidly growing numbers of users in the near future. These represent the markets where you should be present and have your say. How you organize it and who you put in charge are strategic decisions you have to make yourself according to your economic situation. A self-employed salesperson will certainly decide differently to a bigger firm.

Let's return to your potential customers. In a social media sense you may want to "add" those people, that is, invite them to become your "friends", even if a customer relationship has yet to be established. Thus you have a chance—in addition to all the other possibilities described—to build a relationship by posting a status message now and then. You must decide whether or not to keep professional and private contacts apart; this is a very personal decision. If you are interested in my approach, please send me a contact request on Facebook or Xing and/or follow me on Twitter.

USING STATUS MESSAGES TO AROUSE INTEREST

The status messages that you use to turn potentials into customers—or at least to gradually build trust—may include some of the following:

- Report about a project of yours, with due regard to confidentiality
- Innovative services and products you offer
- Critical assessments of certain services geared to enhancing the willingness of people to listen to your recommendations

- Notifications about your lectures, talks etc. to strengthen your reputation
- Developments in your industry that customers may be interested in
- Notifications about your publications
- Information about and links to news on your homepage to strengthen your reputation as an expert
- Exciting pictures of your products, posted with a twinkle in your eye
- If appropriate: recommendations, guestbook entries, and/or positive feedback from your potential customers
- ... now and then, something personal, as you are just a human being, after all ...

As a rule, don't do anything or publish anything you wouldn't like to be associated with in three years time, or at any time, for that matter. The Internet doesn't forget. This shouldn't be a reason, however, for you not to explore these routes in a professional way.

Keep close to your potential customers, using various channels. Sometimes 20, 30, or 50 boosts are required to turn a potential customer into a real customer. Maybe they don't trust you deeply enough yet. Maybe the time has not yet come. Stay present and don't give up.

The following is true of systems and automatisms in general: it is never wrong to directly address someone and suggest cooperating. You have nothing to lose, but everything to win!

HOW SYSTEMATICALLY DO YOU CONTACT YOUR CUSTOMERS BY LETTER?

> Opportunity is everywhere, you only have to recognize it.
> —Sir Charles Clore

THE VERY PERSONAL LETTER

Here's one suggestion: why don't you just send your potential customers a letter, or a prospectus, for that matter? Isn't that the natural thing to do?

Unfortunately, it isn't. Most letters from firms or salespeople to potential customers aren't fit for the job. Senders use them to praise their own achievements to the skies and to promote products 1, 2, and 3. That's exactly what customers have been waiting for.

The glossier and shinier, the faster it goes in the bin, so fast that the short moment it has been in the customers' mind quickly disappears into nirvana. Moreover, most of these letters and prospectuses are of no value to the addressee, so why not throw them away?

Do the opposite: adopt a more individual, and considerate approach. Behind each firm, each service and each product there is a human being: you, for example, the business owner or salesperson. After all, you want to sell something, which puts you among many others who want exactly the same thing. Wouldn't it be better to start out by offering something that is unique, something that people can trust, something as individual and inimitable as yourself?

AVOID USING TRASHY ADVERTISING

What keeps you from introducing yourself in a simple and personal manner rather than reverting to the usual worn-out advertising jargon? Just describe who you are. Tell them about your development, your expertise, your background. Share important insights you have gained. Add something personal you have experienced—the sort of thing you never find in those prospectuses created by marketing professionals. I don't mean that you should write in a nonprofessional style or do it the quick and dirty way. On the contrary, make sure your letters are professional from start to finish. Just make them different, personal and, most importantly, authentic.

Then take this letter and send it in the tried and true form—what we call "snail mail" today—to the potential customers you would like to work with. Include a personal description, perhaps some customer feedback, and possibly one or two features you would like to highlight, chosen based on your experience. Introduce yourself by means of a short anecdote— maybe even the story of something that didn't completely work out but provided you with an important lesson. Close with a clear invitation to work together.

... AND NOTHING HAPPENS ...

It is possible or even likely that your customer will not respond. In that case, wait six or eight weeks, then write another letter to keep the potential customer tuned in. Shift your focus from letter to letter. Write about an experience, about yourself, or about a project, and keep it personal. Avoid too much colour and gloss, and don't go into too much detail concerning your products. Repeat ... and repeat ... and repeat. If it is too much work, remember you don't need to do it yourself.

It was in Stefan Gebhardt-Seele's book *Immer gute Auftragslage* that I first stumbled on the concept of writing very personal letters. True, you could use the auto-responder function and contact your customers via e-mail. I personally, however, prefer the good old letter. Ideally, you may add to each letter a give-away that benefits your customer in some way or another.

Provided you show perseverance, develop a system and don't despair if nothing happens at first, the first customer will eventually call and say, "You have written me several times. Well, here I am ..."

... or something similar. This may not sound very likely, but I assure you it will happen if your letters are good. We have used this strategy as our firm's customer acquisition system since 1991. It has proven effective especially over the long term: we do it again and again. Here is an example of an original letter from our acquisition process—it is confidential, of course.

> **Ladies and Gentlemen, dear prospective customer,** let me introduce myself. My name is Steffen Ritter. I have been the head of the Institut Ritter for more than 20 years. Ever since it was first founded in 1991, my firm has focused almost exclusively on the numbers and results of business owners, salespeople and agents. We have helped them to measurably optimize their business, strengthen their income, and increase liquidity. That is what we do to this day.
>
> Over the years our focus has increasingly shifted to the processes and the development of people working for a sales agency, and to helping them further increase sales and earnings. One particular piece of very honest feedback has encouraged me to commit our institute to dealing with all facets of entrepreneurial activity. Following a consultation, one business owner wrote:
>
> "Dear Mr. Ritter, the things your analysis of our company has brought to the fore are extremely exciting. These are things nobody has told us before. However, and please don't get me wrong, the most important part has happened in the last two hours.
>
> After presenting your analysis you went on to challenge two smaller aspects of our customer care process. You suggested a different approach, communicating it in a very motivating way and training us how to use it. This "bagatelle" has impacted our results ever since. It has been eight years now. Well, business assessment or not, it is all in the processes ..."

The most important learning processes of a firm are those sparked by customer feedback. That is true for us, as well. I hereby apply for the mandate to make your sales agents' processes more professional, systematic and effective. My suggestion is that to begin with I will personally give a motivational talk at one of your annual conventions, followed by customized practical training sessions with my institute's coaches and consultants.

If you are excited by this opportunity, I look forward to your call. If not, I would nonetheless like to thank you for your interest by attaching a practical checklist of processes that, according to our experience, should run automatically and in a professional manner for every sales organization.

For further information please call me (tel. +49 (0) 3464 573980).

Best regards,
Steffen Ritter
Managing Director, Institut Ritter GmbH

PS: For more boosts please visit www.ritterblog.de!

This was one of our firm's letters. Is it possible to write this way? Should you write about having learned this or that? Wouldn't it be better to imply that you have always been perfect? That is certainly a matter of preference and it is up to you to decide.

Today, as one would say in German, there is more "Schein" than "Sein", more pretentions and less of the real thing—especially in the world of marketing. Stand out, be different!

If you contact your potential customers on a regular basis to draw their attention to how exciting you are, it is only a matter of time before your efforts will pay off.

PART C — SERVICING AND DEVELOPING

HOW SYSTEMATICALLY DO YOU CATEGORIZE YOUR CUSTOMERS?

> To organize means to prevent events from following their natural course and people from acting on their own will.
> —Helmar Nahr

PREREQUISITES FOR SUCCESS

Now the exciting part begins. Having discussed all the pros and cons of class A and class C customers, let's get to the crunch. How do you categorize your customers?

Here are some considerations you should take into account:

- If you are going to categorize your customers without giving it much thought and continue as before, you may as well not do it at all.
- Clearly highlight your customer classes in your customer software, so that you and your people instantly know who belongs to which class.
- Make sure your customer classes are automatically selectable in your customer software, so that customers can be cared for according to which class they belong to.
- As customers develop and customer values change, make sure customer classes can be subsequently changed also.
- If you have people working for you, make sure you have everybody on board. Explain why it is important, speak about concerns and provide assistance.

GOOD CUSTOMERS, BAD CUSTOMERS

Whilst categorizing your customers you may ask yourself, "What exactly is a 'bad' customer?" Although a "bad" customer in the proper sense may not exist, the following traits and attributes could lead in that direction:

- Costs a lot of time, doesn't buy anything
- Results in a negative contribution margin
- Doesn't pay in time
- Must be sent payment reminders
- Complains frequently
- Always tries to renegotiate prices
- "Harms" the company

In my book *Die Entwicklung Ihres Unternehmens* I recommended the following four classes of customer:

- **Class A customers**
  These are customers creating solid revenues for your company, with potential for further development.

- **Class B customers**
  These are customers also creating solid revenues, but with little or no potential for further development.

- **Class C customers**
  These are customers only marginally contributing to your revenues. They show little or no interest in developing the business

relationship further, or show some or all of the traits of "bad" customers, see above.

- **Class N customers**
  N stands for "no classification". These customers don't yet contribute to your revenues to any extent. It remains to be seen, however, whether or not they have potential for further development, so they have not yet been classified.

Make sure your customer classification is the first step in a sophisticated care system, which enables you to provide customers with a differentiated care service based on economically sound sales.

HOW SYSTEMATICALLY DO YOUR CLASS C CUSTOMERS GENERATE PROFIT?

He who wishes to live long must serve, but he who wishes to rule does not live long.
—Hermann Hesse

DIFFERENTIATE BETWEEN CUSTOMER CLASSES

Let's talk about your "bad" customers, those who aren't that bad at all if you deal with them accordingly. Online stores often categorize customers as they place their very first order. A finely-tuned assessment algorithm estimates the costs and sales a new customer is likely to generate. This classification is the basis for all internal processes that follow.

With some customers, you will "know" right from the beginning whether or not they have potential. Most of the time you are right, but sometimes things turn out quite differently. The development of a customer relationship depends upon too many parameters to provide 100 percent certainty. That is not the point, however.

By classifying your customers as described above you are able to identify your class C customers. These are customers who, for instance,

- generate little profit compared to other customers
- seem to have little potential for development
- cost a lot of time whilst generating little or no profit

For you to be able to focus on customers who generate profit for your company, have potential for development, and can recommend you to an exiting clientele, you have to provide customers not fitting this description with a different, leaner form of customer care. There are essentially two ways to provide customer care:

- The active approach, where you take the initiative to reach out to the customer
- The reactive approach, where you wait for the customer to reach out to you

With class C customers, you may decide to stop actively reaching out to them, thus reacting only if they reach out to you. In this case, you must further decide how to respond, compared to your response to other customers such as those of class A. This differentiation may be based on these criteria:

- How long does it take for you to process a request?
- Who will be in charge of processing a request?

Such differentiation may at first seem to contradict the very principles of service, but let me repeat: caring for all customers in the same manner often results in all customers being given a level of care that is average at best. It is important that you use your resources to generate maximum value for your customers with respect to your business, and possibly your employees' workforce.

DEVELOP CLASS C CUSTOMERS

No customer classification should be carved in stone, as even class C customers may develop. That is the reason why active forms of customer care shouldn't be ruled out even for class C customers. Keep these lean, however, in order not to compromise the profitability of your business. Send them your newsletter, but send it via e-mail (with class A customers receiving a hard copy).

Let them access you by phone, but limit the hours of accessibility (as compared to class A customers). Offer appointments, but only on your premises (with class A customers being offered appointments on their premises, too). Tailor your own offerings based on the specifics of your industry. There are lots of options. It's worth thinking about.

Don't turn into a reactive servant, obsequiously doing whatever your customers ask you to do, whether or not you and your business can afford it. Sooner or later you won't be able to provide them any service whatsoever, as your company will have ceased to exist.

HOW SYSTEMATICALLY DO YOU SERVICE YOUR CLASS A CUSTOMERS?

Turn your company into the most exciting place in the world.
—Jack Welch

AN EXCELLENT START IS FOLLOWED BY DOLDRUMS?

When it comes to class C customers, make sure you adjust your service level if you don't want to jeopardize your already small profit.

Now let's talk about your class A customers. Suppose you have won a really great customer. That is when consultancy work gets truly exciting. Many business owners and salespeople play in the Champions' League of winning customers. When it comes to caring for them, however, they play in the regional league at best.

Now that you have done such a good job in recruiting your new customer, are you ready for and, most importantly, capable of following up with a truly professional customer service. Or does your strength lie in the ability to initiate cooperation, rather than in keeping it up in the long run?

To be able to care for your customers in the best possible way, you need a plan. Replace the salesperson's intuition with a systematic sequence of steps. That way, you won't wake up at 3.27 a.m. thinking of Smith, your class A customer from Chapter 1 anymore. Now, it is your system that does the thinking for you.

WHAT EXACTLY ARE YOU GOING TO DO WHEN? AND HOW?

More specifically, do you have people working with you? Who will be in charge of what? And when? In order to be able to sustainably deliver professional class-A customer care, this is an important first step.

Unless you take care of this first step, you won't provide your class A customers with a "somewhat better" service unless, by chance, you have some spare time, sense an itching in your nose, or feel obliged by the approach of Christmas to signal your customers that you are still there for them—class-A customer care powered by a guilty conscience ...

Here are some suggestions on how to provide value to your class A customers on a regular basis:

- Send newsletters (hard copy or e-mail): quarterly, for instance.
- Reach out to customers, giving them "huddle calls" at fixed intervals
- Make an offer, or ask your customers how and how often they want you to reach out to them
- Without the customers requesting it, create situation and needs analyses and communicate these when, for instance, products are updated or changes take effect.
- Stage a worthwhile and unusual annual event as an "upgrade" for class A customers.
- Cross-link your class A customers in order to promote their businesses (thereby providing more than average value).
- Offer preferential service to special customers by providing longer hours of accessibility and/or a special hotline.
- Offer preferential service by assigning each customer their "own" consultant.
- Offer preferential service by reducing response times.
- Improve cost-benefit ratio by offering extensive collaboration.
- Pay special attention once a year (it doesn't have to be at Christmas time).
- Try your best to give customers the appointment they wish (in terms of time and location).

- Offer clearly-defined 360-degree care, which may also include unusual additional services.
- Ask customers individually about their satisfaction, their needs and wishes. Make sure you don't annoy them.
- Offer special care as a guaranteed service.
- Offer special information via a separate log in on your homepage.
- Underline special customer status by handing out a golden customer card (possibly with top services listed on the back)

You may have quite different ideas to suit your particular situation. Take the above suggestions as a starting point. The more specific your approach, however, the better and more authentic it will be. In particular, think about the capabilities and special features of your services. What are your unique characteristics?

Are you able to provide a special kind of customer care that highlights these characteristics? Often, this may be the starting point for successful networking activity. Doing something for your community is a quick and straightforward way to spread the word. Local media are likely to report on it—unlike events staged for business purposes only, which don't justify coverage.

WRITE IT DOWN, COMMIT TO IT, REPEAT ...

As I mentioned earlier, it is important that you write your intention down, to make sure you will follow through. Define who will be in charge. Some of the activities can certainly be outsourced. A systematic approach doesn't necessarily require you to do everything yourself. On the contrary, entrepreneurship means being able to delegate tasks, so you can focus on more profitable activities, or even not contribute at all for a while.

Start only what you can keep up. If you do something special once, only to fall back to five years of no care, your class A customers will be even more acutely aware of it.

HOW SYSTEMATICALLY DO YOU DEVELOP YOUR POTENTIAL CUSTOMERS?

> I think luck is the sense to recognize an opportunity
> and the ability to take advantage of it.
> —Samuel Goldwyn

"NEITHER-NOR CUSTOMERS"

Now that we have talked about class A and class C customers, let's discuss those customers who are neither A nor C. Customers who are not very profitable at the moment, but do have the potential for further development, tend to slip through the net, as in the daily course of events nobody knows exactly which class they belong to. As a consequence, all customers are treated equally, resulting in lots of work and almost no time left for systematically realizing customers' potential.

Customers with potential include class B customers who are already creating some profit while giving rise to hopes for more, as well as class N customers (not yet categorized) who are creating little or no profit for the time being, but possibly have the potential for more in the future. Once again, we can see that the process of systematically developing and realizing potential has two dimensions: the reactive and the pro-active.

REACTIVE SYSTEMS

If an existing customer who has potential—at least on paper—reaches out to you by phone or by paying you a visit, it is your job to instantly recognize that opportunity. Once the customer count goes up, this becomes nearly impossible without the use of a computer database with customer entries appropriately marked. It is therefore important that you acquire the habit of immediately consulting your program and acting accordingly.

A statement like "I'm glad you called. I just saw a mark in your customer file. We were planning to get in touch with you" is one way to steer the conversation in the right direction right from the beginning. You may, however, choose a completely different form, such as:

- a proposal providing additional value
- statutory changes
- a short-term promotional event
- special benefits, etc.

This approach can help you to pro-actively arouse curiosity and interest. A customer who reaches out to you is tuned in at that moment, so he or she tends to be more open to have a conversation than if caught off guard and unprepared.

It is important to establish the quick glance at the customer class as a routine step, as a fixed habit. If people working for you are involved, make sure they act in the same way. The important thing is to develop and to set down in writing a consistent approach that is binding for everybody involved. All employees should have the opportunity to practice this behaviour in an authentic setting, repeating it many times.

PRO-ACTIVE SYSTEMS

The second dimension is pro-actively reaching out to customers. This is equally important, as not all of your potential customers will take the initiative to get in touch with you. Depending on your strategy and your industry, there are several approaches that could be used, such as:

- special products adding to the existing offer
- special offers available exclusively to a small circle of customers
- an offer of 360-degree counselling, including special benefits, extras and/or discounts

How you proceed depends on your personal strategy. If you actively reach out to the customer, you should make a detailed note in your customer system of when and why you contacted the customer to make sure you don't contact them too often, which may not be helpful and might even annoy them.

As potential customers may include class B (those already creating considerable profit) as well as class N customers (not yet categorized), different approaches are recommended. Most importantly, maintain customer files carefully to make sure you don't tell them the same things over and over again. After all, this seems to work for Starbucks! yThere, at least, I haven't seen a front line employee reaching for my customer file after I said my name was Steffen.

NOT SO FAST: CLASS N BECOMES CLASS C

Suppose you have tried several times to develop a class N customer—who, however, categorically refuses to intensify their collaboration with you, thus demonstrating their lack of confidence in a deepened relationship. This would be reason enough to classify them as a class C customer. Be careful not to interpret a first "no" as a definite rejection. Perhaps your first attempt just came at the wrong moment—something I am sure you know all too well. Although you are generally open to advances, there may be times when you can't be bothered ...

HOW SYSTEMATICALLY DO YOU FOLLOW UP?

> Pleasant memories have to be arranged for in
> advance.
> —Paul Hörbiger

AFTER THE SALES IS BEFORE THE SALES

You can assign your customers to different groups or classes depending on how profitable they are and how much potential they have. So far so good: as soon as such a classification exists, a systematic approach becomes possible, the significance of which cannot be overestimated.

Many business owners and many salespeople stop talking to a customer after closing one or more deals with them. The contract has been signed and goods and services have been delivered, so the task has been "completed." Some friendly parting words and that's it.

This may seem logical insofar as this ending was the object of the exercise. In terms of a systematic approach, however, it doesn't go far enough. The positive mood of a successful deal provides an excellent opportunity for initiating the subsequent service arrangement, or even future deals. This is also a good way of strengthening your business: it allows you to be seen as a salesperson or a company that keeps their word and remains present. Make sure, however, that you do remain present ...

Ideally, once you have identified customer classes, you will know when it is best for both sides to get in touch again. Since follow-up care shouldn't be a kind of charity, you ultimately have to plan the rhythms for your various customer classes from an economic point of view as well.

Which customers should have their next appointment scheduled a year from now? For which customers would a quarterly rhythm be more appropriate? When is a customer due for a follow-up? Conversely, which customers should only be entitled to reactive care, so that no follow-up is needed?

Some businesses have had success in involving their customers in the decision process. Explain to them what kind of service and care package you are offering, and seek their consent. Make it clear why this follow-up care is so important. Let your customers sense its importance, and provide that feeling of "we are there for you".

NO FOLLOW-UP? GROSSLY NEGLIGENT ...

After successfully concluding a deal, you mustn't let your customer disappear in the depth of your customer bucket (remember the green frogs?). If you do, you'll soon become the servant of those insisting on being cared for (remember Roth?). You'll invest more time and energy in servicing them than is in any way justified, whilst forgetting about and postponing those who had once paid for being cared for (remember Smith?). As far as your business and your sales activities are concerned, such behaviour is grossly negligent. It is a sin against your own future.

By leaving the thinking to your follow-up system you get a good night's sleep whilst making sure that your customers are appropriately cared for. To establish such a thinking system you first have to do some thinking yourself. How often do you want to contact which customers? When can you be helpful to them by providing important information? At what intervals should you revisit deals already concluded? How often do new developments need to be kept track of?

Reasons to reach out to customers may include legislative decisions, new products, interesting follow-up, add-on or servicing products, and any new offers you want to make on your part. The possible reasons are as manifold as the branches that you, my dear readers, are active in. Ultimately, it is all about deepening and strengthening your business relationships with customers. It is all about a systematic approach to selling.

Selling without a systematic follow-up process is selling without a plan, so be sure to have your systems in place! If not, you will risk seeing each customer only once. You will have to arbitrarily decide which frog is due for a follow-up and which frog has to climb the ladder on their own initiative, leaving the rest uncared-for and sitting in the depths of your bucket.

HOW SYSTEMATICALLY DO YOU CONTINUE TO CREATE VALUE FOR YOUR CUSTOMERS?

> Only the ideas we actually live are of any value.
> —Hermann Hesse

HOW TO CREATE REAL VALUE FOR YOUR CUSTOMERS

In the preceding sections, I have mentioned the need to attract attention. Additionally, in the context of recruiting potential customers, I mentioned auto-responders as a means of reminding customers of your continued presence. I now want to tackle this topic from a different perspective.

An excellent way to turn potentials into customers and develop and retain your existing customers is to provide them with value on a regular basis. To paraphrase John F. Kennedy: "Ask not what your customers can do for you—ask what you can do for your customers."

Consistently and systematically providing value to your existing customers as well as your prospective customers should be a distinctive feature of your business. You should simply provide value to everyone that you would like to be in business with. Be exciting, provide valuable information and insight, and become the companion your customers and prospective customers would like to have contact with.

By doing so, you will strengthen your existing customer relationships. Your potential customers will, when the need arises, prefer to work with you, their valuable partner, rather than with any other supplier. For this to happen, you must take care to provide value for more than charitable purposes, by regularly reminding them of what you have to offer. If not, you may as well reclassify your business as a "charity".

EXAMPLES OF HOW TO CREATE VALUE FOR YOUR CUSTOMERS

How can you provide value? How can you be really helpful? Here are some ideas to adapt to your business and your industry. Not all of them will be appropriate, since solutions have to be authentic and suitable to your situation. It has to be something you like to do, so in the long term it won't be difficult for you to maintain. If there is even just one idea that suits you, it is enough. Here are my examples:

- Help your private customers save money. Provide tips and boosts, if appropriately related to your products.
- Help your corporate customer to be successful by recommending, linking to, and advertising them.
- Provide your customer with impartial checklists, along with your honest recommendations in order to aid in their decision making.

- Make sure your product prospectuses offer some value, and a good reason for the customer to keep them rather than dump them right away.
- Regularly offer valuable information and comprehensive know-how on your homepage.
- Establish a community so that your customers may learn from each other.
- Offer input on various communication channels. Exploit the potential of the broad spectrum of social media platforms.
- Be a trend scout for your customers, so that your contact is a guarantee for being well informed.
- Make work easier for your customers. Do things for them your competitors wouldn't do.
- Become a hub for your target group by linking to everybody and proving yourself a true expert.
- Be sure that you are well-known and renowned, so that working with you is beneficial to their image.
- Continue to develop your products and services, so that customers know they are at the cutting edge.
- Provide your customers with a guarantee of what they can expect when working with you. Create confidence by confirming your services in written form.
- Provide first-class customers with special benefits as a reward for doing a lot of business with you.

These are just a few examples. Modify and adapt ideas to your situation. You don't have to implement all of them. Industries and strategies tend to be quite different, so some of these suggestions may not fit your circumstances. Consider brainstorming with your people, colleagues, or partners, or appoint a consultancy firm specialized in your industry.

Ultimately, make sure you don't just set up a business and wait for customers to come. Ask from your customers' perspective. What would be of value to them? The better you can answer this question, the more successful you will be. As soon as you have your own approach, start to do it again and again.

Systemize and develop the process. Keep an eye on the results of what you do, so that you may continue to do the right things. Monitor technological developments. Nothing is set in stone, the market decides. That was true yesterday, it is true today, and it will be true tomorrow.

PART D — CUSTOMER LOYALTY AND RECOMMENDATION

HOW SYSTEMATICALLY DO YOUR CUSTOMERS RECOMMEND YOU TO OTHERS?

> Nothing great was ever achieved without enthusiasm.
> —Ralph Waldo Emerson

THE TROUBLE WITH RECOMMENDATIONS

You have won customers and done a great job of caring for them? That is good. Did it all happen as the result of a well-thought-out, autonomous system? Then that is even better. But don't be satisfied too soon.

The customers who most value your quality are your most precious assets, so benefit from them. From the title of this section, you certainly know what I'm talking about. That is, I want you to aim to get customers to explicitly recommend your services!

Now you may think, "That is what I have tried to achieve from time to time, but with no success ..." Be that as it may, however, could it be that, once again, you weren't successful due to the lack of a systematic approach?

Recommendations sometimes smack of "they don't have enough customers, so they depend on this. Maybe, they just aren't as good ..." Is that what you think yourself, and so you hesitate to ask your customer to recommend you to others, fearing they might come to the same conclusion? Take a different approach, do it better!

Your attitude should be that you don't need it. Maybe this sounds familiar to you. Whenever there is less need for additional sales, things pan out well. I think it is important not to let others feel that you are in urgent need of new customers. Instead, appreciate any new recommendation, and welcome your new customer in a relaxed way.

There are several ways to encourage satisfied customers to recommend you to others. You may, for example, offer your best customers—those who you want to recommend you—a special, exclusive service. This could be a "gold card" combined with high-value services. You may also offer your best customers premium access to your homepage whilst providing valuable boosts and information relating to your product or service. How about organizing a special event exclusively for your very best customers?

Then, as a next step, you may inform your customer:

> Mr. Jones, I am glad that we do business together. As our valued customer, you will receive our gold card granting you access to special services such as ... By the way, you may share these benefits with one other party. Simply give us their name, and they will then receive their own gold card. Whilst there is no obligation for this person to become our customer, he or she will be entitled to all of the same services as you. We would like to let our service speak for itself, so we won't get in touch before the card expires.

THE TROUBLE WITH RECOMMENDATIONS

For you and many others, such an approach may be too defensive and too slow—so step it up a gear and adapt it to your particular genius. By the way, success comes with consistency and establishing a system. I often hear, "Well, that way it would take me a year to get a new customer, if at all ..." Right, then—if you provide your special customers with special services all year long, they will start to arrive even earlier on their own initiative.

It is your job to develop a system that enables you to offer valuable benefits in advance and to excel in doing so. Your customer who is doing the recommending will have the advantage of being in a position to offer something valuable to others. More precisely, to exactly one other person, whom they have to choose. This is the crucial point. Make sure that your recommending customer can feel like a hero, as that is one of the reasons, perhaps even the only reason, for him to recommend you.

In the eyes of your customer, by introducing this limitation, you become the one who has something to offer rather than the one begging for a recommendation. That is exactly the point. You, the business owner or salesperson, should follow the basic rule of selling. The best way to win new customers is to provide them with value before they actually become your customers. Thus you make yourself a name and build trust. Reputation and trust are the best possible basis for developing a prosperous customer relationship.

To keep in mind the objective of this book, let me repeat: it is your job to systemize an approach similar to the one presented on these pages. Only then can the underlying strategy unfold its potential. Make sure that a statement like "this is the way we always do it" gets others unfailingly enthusiastic about your business. Moreover, if there is something that "is not possible in my business or industry", try to think positively about a way that it could be done. By the way, this is exactly the starting point of an entrepreneur ...

HOW SYSTEMATICALLY DO YOU OFFER EXTRAS TO YOUR CUSTOMERS?

> Ducks lay eggs discreetly, on the other hand a chicken makes noise so the whole estate can hear. What is the result? The whole world eats chicken eggs, just a few use duck eggs.
> —Henry Ford

CUSTOMER BONDING VIA SPECIALS

A moment ago we talked about exclusive services such as gold cards. Wasn't that enough? Is there a need for more specials? Isn't it enough to deliver first-class work? Isn't it enough to provide the best products? Well, that is certainly important. It provides the foundation for being consistently present in the market. True customer bonding, however, often requires you to go one step further.

It is essential that you speak not only to your customer's mind, but also to his heart. Try to touch him there and give him the feeling of being well cared for. Exclusive services as described in the previous section are helpful, but you really should go one step further and reach out to his heart. Make sure your customer is truly "fond" of you and your business. This may sound rather naive, but it is the success formula of many a business and many a salesperson.

To make sure customers remain loyal in the long run, it is useful to offer them unexpected specials from time to time. These may be activities and ideas showing them that you have them in mind—not as a burden, but as the focus of whatever you do. The question is: what can you do on a regular basis to surprise your customers, strengthen their loyalty, and encourage them to recommend you to others?

Let's start at the beginning again. As a norm, you are good and you and your products and services are reliable and high quality. Does this mean there is someone who recommends you or talks about you to others? Maybe. To really stand out, you should do something extraordinary from time to time.

When I say "from time to time", I mean regularly, in fixed intervals: annually, for instance. Here too, go for the systematic approach. By doing so, you demonstrate reliability and consistency even in these not completely business-related areas. When I say extraordinary it may well be something slightly crazy, even if the main part of your work tends to be rather serious. It makes you stand out, arousing people's curiosity by giving them something to talk about or maybe even write about.

To make these ideas tangible, I am going to give you some examples. However, treat them with tolerance, please. Again, they aren't necessarily applicable to your situation, and they won't necessarily be to your liking. I would be content if you took this chance to just think about them and gradually derive and develop your own ideas.

THE SMALL EVENTS

- Once a year, organize "the slightly different sightseeing tour" in your region, exclusively for your customers and, of course, the media. Below ground, hidden places you normally wouldn't get access to, or forgotten areas ... with an expert in history to share knowledge.

- Invite your customers to a movie preview with Coke and popcorn two weeks before the premiere.
- Organize a family miniature golf event in your community, and donate the proceeds to charity.
- Invite your customers to chop down their own Christmas tree in the Advent season, or invite them for brunch on a Saturday morning, and offer each top customer a tree to take home.
- Organize an Easter walk for families and children, with little surprises along the way.
- Organize guided autumn hikes to local attractions, and make sure that the media take note. Prepare a photo album of the event and give it to your customers.
- Bring your customers primroses as soon as they are available, or other spring flowers. These only cost a few cents, but nevertheless are a nice surprise.

Do something that is typical of you and your team. I know a company that annually organizes raft rides for their top customers and business partners, with lunch and music. Do something authentic that customers will talk about and wish to participate in repeatedly. Establish a tradition, your own tradition, something beyond the usual.

This is not all that crazy, of course. You could, for instance, organize a crazy sport event; however, this would limit the number of eligible participants. It's completely up to you. It ultimately depends on your target group. Think about it, think laterally, be different, and don't hesitate to be a little unusual. Pull it off ...

Just to be sure, keep delivering first-class products and services in your primary field, and you will be on the right track!

HOW SYSTEMATICALLY DO YOU DEAL WITH CUSTOMER DEFECTION?

> Usually, when two divorce, one suffers
> somewhat more.
> —Wilhelm Busch

IT'S YOUR CUSTOMER WHO GIVES YOU THE MOST IMPORTANT LESSON

What is positive about a customer who defects? Nothing, at least at first sight. You can, however, learn something from it. Defections are a highly valuable lesson for you and your business. Of course, not every defection comes as a cancellation of a membership or a termination of a contract. Sometimes a customer who has been loyal so far suddenly stays away, or a customer buys just once from you and doesn't come back later, even though that is not in line with your business concept. In this book, for the purpose of generalization, I'll speak of "defection" in each of these cases. Let's consider some of the possible options and variations.

VARIATION 1: A LOSS-GENERATING CUSTOMER DEFECTS

A customer may leave who hasn't been profitable for your business for years. I am sure you know such customers. Initially they may have brought you a tiny profit, but then they just produced a significant amount of questions and inquiries—enough to keep two of your people busy, with possibly dozens of hours invested by yourself, the boss.

One might ask, of course: why didn't you develop that loss-generating customer of yours, or why didn't you use your systems to provide him with a leaner care scheme? Was it because of hope—which, notoriously, dies last? Perhaps you didn't notice? Has there been an error in your system? Are customers like that simply part of the game?

These are questions you have to answer for yourself. Even if it involves a customer who bought a low level of care, how tolerant are you with business relationships that do not yield profit? Even if the defecting customer has not generated any profit in the first place, you should definitely be interested in knowing why they don't want to cooperate any longer.

VARIATION 2: A PROFIT-GENERATING CUSTOMER DEFECTS

This is annoying, of course, but there is no way to make sure that no single customer will leave you. Even if your level of customer care has been consistently above average, a customer who apparently has been happy so far may defect. Sometimes there are reasons and motives you can't do anything about; however, that's the exception. Try to take a professional perspective. Your defecting customer is the best business consultant you can find, especially if they have been generating profits for you.

The following wording, for instance, may be helpful in an industry where it is common to close long-term contracts, such as copy machine maintenance, winter services, or grave maintenance. Whilst your aim should be to win the customer back, the first step is to understand their reasons for leaving you. Don't rely on the written form, and don't hide behind letters and mail. Speak with your customer face to face, or, at least, talk to him or her on the phone.

> Mr. Jones, you've terminated your contract with us, so that's why I'm calling. It is extremely rare for a customer to leave us, so it's important for me to understand how we could have done better, especially with you, as we highly value your opinion.

Strike up a conversation with your customer that is free of blame. It is not just about winning him back, but first and foremost about understanding the reasons why he defected. Don't discuss these reasons. Your customer is right anyway, at least in their own perception. Don't argue, and don't try to prove them wrong. Finish your learning session with your "business consultant" with some friendly remarks such as:

> Mr. Jones, I thank you for the open and honest conversation.
> I value your judgment, and you have helped me a lot.

Use wording similar to this, especially if your customer has been objective and fair. Make sure you leave your customer with a good feeling. It's a pity that defecting customers are rarely dealt with in such a manner. You, on the other hand, may get valuable insights. In a follow-up conversation, having internalized all the information, you may then launch an attempt to win your customer back.

> Mr. Jones, I thank you again for the pleasant and open conversation and for the time spent. I'd very much like to continue our collaboration and put forward a proposal on how that could be done. Would you be prepared to give me that chance?

In this situation, it is particularly important for you to sound authentic if you want to be successful. So choose your words carefully and don't talk in a stilted manner. Remember that you have nothing to lose. In fact, this customer has been lost already.

What's important is not just to strike up a conversation but to ask the reasons for defecting. Be prepared to listen and to learn. These reasons may be down to you and to your business. There is always room for improvement.

4.

HOW TO CREATE NEW HABITS

HOW STANDARD PRACTICES MAKE YOUR WORK AND LIFE EASIER

> Simple can be harder than complex: you have to work hard to get your thinking clean to make it simple. But it's worth it in the end because once you get there, you can move mountains.
> —Steve Jobs

HOIST YOUR STANDARD

In the preceding chapters, I have given examples of processes that are worth standardizing. The aim of establishing standard practices is to perform tasks in a consistent manner, to make these tasks easy and predictable. Moreover, it is easy to develop (good) habits in a standardized atmosphere. You simply do what you always do. If you do it right, these habits will almost automatically lead to success.

Wikipedia says, "A standard practice or procedure gives a set of instructions for performing operations or functions."

A note on the origin of the word "standard": the English royal standards are occasionally mentioned. In the case of those bearing the king's name and emblem, certain norms were seen as valid. The standard was an army flag fixed to a pole, visible from afar so that squads and units knew where to collect. Think about today's tourist guides who hoist their employer's "standard" to prevent their protégés from losing sight of them.

And so "standard" stands for simplifying, bringing together, normalizing and adopting a consistent approach. Establishing and adopting standard practices may bring about the following advantages:

- By repeatedly performing certain practices and procedures, you develop positive habits.
- It becomes easier for you to start performing a task, as there is no need to develop a new concept.
- With each repetition you become more confident.
- By repeating the same task over and over again you are able to increase efficiency and make better use of your personal experience.
- It becomes easier for you to guarantee a consistently high quality.
- It is easier for you to delegate tasks, as standards are more easily taught, especially when put into written form.
- By delegating standardized tasks to your people you free time to devote to new, more valuable tasks.
- You can include crucial tasks in your personal system and develop them into habits, thereby securing lasting success.
- You can communicate your standard practices to your customers as guaranteed services since you would reliably adhere to them.

As you see, standard practices come with quite a number of advantages. However, it is not so easy to establish standard practices. That is ultimately because your old habits are so powerful that they dominate everything new. Consistency and persistence are therefore required, so you won't give up at half-time when the old habit appears to still be dominating the match.

WHY MANY PEOPLE DON'T LIKE STANDARD PRACTICES

> I often wish people would talk less and come to the point.
> —Cyril Northcote Parkinson

STANDARD PRACTICES HAVE A LOW THRILL FACTOR AT FIRST

It would be fatal to believe that standard practices are always enthusiastically accepted. Often the contrary is the case. Most business owners, salespeople, office workers and others concerned prefer to work on an individual basis. Their mantra is to specifically respond to each situation and to each particular customer.

A standard practice or procedure supposedly presses everything into a mould or a fixed approach. Individuality may fall by the wayside, allowing compromise to rule. Can that be good? Doesn't successful sales activity require customer needs to be maximally attended to and benefits offered on an individual basis? Fair enough, so such concerns have to be taken seriously. There are some rules:

- Standard practices must make things easier rather than more complicated.
- Standard practices must assist rather than interfere with the consultant work.
- Standard practices must benefit customers rather than impede customer service.
- Standard practices must boost sales rather than produce more administration work.
- Standard practices must be self-evident rather than rocket science.

For instance, if you want to use a checklist for interrogating and analyzing customer needs on a regular basis, this list mustn't contain questions without relevance, or else users will soon return to the previous practice of analyzing needs without reference to a unified checklist.

If you want to know the class of a calling customer so that you may choose a standardized approach depending on which class the customer belongs to, such information must be quickly accessible without the need for additional clicks, or else you will soon be tempted to avoid this cumbersome inquiry because it makes the internal process more difficult.

PRECLUDE TRAILS

If a certain standard practice doesn't prove helpful once it is established, do not despair. Instead, learn from it, thereby gaining valuable experience. Imagine a municipal park in which new footpaths have been laid. Sometimes these paths are terribly impractical, so visitors start to look for shortcuts which lead to the emergence of new trails.

Standard practices, like new but impractical paths, tend to be ignored if they

- do not bring about significant improvements,
- do not help to save time,
- are of no recognizable benefit,

but instead require users to

- give up familiar old habits,
- adapt to new, complicated processes, and
- forgo their individuality.

Make sure you introduce standard practices that are simple and bring about improvements, so that results prove their usefulness.

IT'S THE WHAT RATHER THAN THE HOW: STANDARDIZING THE RIGHT THINGS

> If you keep your focus, eventually your focus
> will keep you.
> —Stephen King

WHAT IS YOUR GOAL?

In the establishing of standard practices for your business, the question of "how to" arises. What would be the best way? What would be the easiest way? Often, however, whilst asking about the "how", people forget to ask what the "what" was in the first place. Which tasks will enable you to achieve your goals?

We live in a world that is optimized for efficiency. Everything is implemented as economically as possible. Although the conscious use of resources requires such an approach let me question the tasks on your to-do list. Do they really enable you to achieve your goals, or do they just fill your days? Being wildly busy with operational tasks most of the day is not an expression of diligence, but rather an expression of being too lazy about thinking.

I'm sure you have a lot of tasks on your to-do list that are not conducive to your goals. These tasks won't get better by performing them as economically as possible. It is even worse if these tasks occupy a major part of your day. And in this case, time management that helps you to do more in less time is of no use, either. There is only one solution, and that is to eliminate all tasks that do not help to achieve your goals.

Effectiveness is all about helping you to achieve your goals. Efficiency is all about performing tasks as economically as possible. When it comes to achieving your goals, effectiveness is more important than efficiency. The "what" beats the "how".

Make sure you know which tasks contribute most to achieving your goals before you decide about the "how". Before you can systemize, standardize, and automate, you have to think. You will have to ask yourself where you want to go. Which goal do you want to achieve by developing your business and your selling activity?

DO YOU KNOW YOUR 20 PERCENT?

I'd like to draw your attention to an inconspicuous "law." It is an economic principle that almost everybody in the business of sales is familiar with. This is the 80-20 rule suggested by the Italian engineer Vilfredo Frederico Pareto (1848-1923), according to which 80 percent of the output of a project is produced in 20 percent of the total time invested into the project. The remaining 80 percent of the time is necessary to produce the remaining 20 percent of the output.

Apply this concept to your business. Doing this repeatedly—and often unconsciously—is one of the secrets to success of most successful salespeople. Some questions may help you get started:

- Which 20 percent of your customers create 80 percent of your sales?
- Which 20 percent of your products yield 80 percent of your income?
- Which 20 percent of your daily work directly or indirectly causes 80 percent of your success?
- Which 20 percent of your people (including yourself, the owner) achieve 80 percent of your selling success?
- Which 20 percent of your office hours are used by 80 percent of your customers?
- Which 20 percent of your IT applications do you use in 80 percent of your business activities?

Economically, it makes a lot of sense to focus on your 20 percent—in whatever context.

THE IMPORTANT TASKS MUST RUN AUTOMATICALLY

Tasks and activities with the following attributes are perfectly suited to being standardized:

- **Tasks of elementary importance**
  Standardization helps turn tasks into habits or automatisms. Of course, that is particularly important with tasks that are crucial for your success.
- **Recurring important tasks**
  Constantly recurring tasks should be realized in a particularly energy-efficient way. Here, standard practices have a great impact. From an economic perspective, automation can lead to maximum efficiency.
- **Important tasks that consume a lot of time and effort**
  For tasks requiring huge amounts of time and effort on a regular basis, standardization can help streamline the processes involved. Often the need to reinvent the wheel is the main source of inefficiency.

With regard to the Pareto principle, the core question to be asked about a task is whether it significantly contributes to the selling success or service quality, which will hopefully lead to further selling success. Does a task belong to the 20 percent responsible for 80 percent of your success? A high frequency of occurrence and the amount of effort required aren't enough to justify the existence of the task. A thorough analysis may even result in the complete elimination of such a task.

Let's consider an example. A salesperson records customer follow-up data not only in the digital customer database but also in a personal handwritten calendar. Double-entry bookkeeping safeguards important data. However, with reasonable backup systems, it is superfluous, no matter how much standardization has been put into effect.

THE SMALL DIFFERENCE

So, remain aware of the two terms efficiency and effectiveness. Efficiency is a measure of economic viability, and effectiveness is the ratio between the status quo and the defined goal.

Here is another example. Suppose there is quite an efficient way to gain a new customer for your product. However, in the long run this customer creates more expenses than revenues. If your aim is to work with customers who create a profit, winning this customer is not effective in the first place as you fail your aim. Standardizing and automating the process of winning unprofitable customers would in fact be counterproductive.

WHAT ABOUT YOUR 80 PERCENT?

Based on those 20 percent of tasks significantly contributing to your success, there arises the question what to do with the remaining 80 percent. Should you just get rid of them? Perhaps you should. At least, there are always three possible approaches:

- Eliminate
- Delegate
- Automate

With regard to your to-do list, this means:

- Eliminate rigorously whatever does not directly, or indirectly, contribute to your success.
- Rigorously delegate those tasks that, whilst being inevitable, are not worth your precious time.
- Automate whatever can be automated.

With regard to the customers you care for:

- Part company in a friendly manner with customers who create more expenses than revenue in the long run, but refuse to enter into a deeper, more profitable business relationship.

- Make sure customers that are neither actually nor potentially profitable but form a solid base of your business are cared for by less expensive people.
- Be sure to simplify and automate the customer care process using standard practices, so that you are able, even with limited resources, to provide systematic customer care.

THE MIRACLE OF ATTENTION

This is anything but easy. Daily routine catches up with you in no time, even if you have determined your "what" and know which tasks and customers will bring you closer to your goals. It is now time to focus.

We live in an era of distraction. Our daily life is characterized by interruptions. Mail is arriving continuously rather than once a day. Even after office hours it keeps arriving on our smartphones, and even if mail reception is disabled, text messages come through.

Faxes emerge from buzzing machines, or appear silently on computer screens. There are interruptions every minute. Working on a single task for longer stretches of time is completely out of fashion. Communication follows a 140-character rhythm. Quick, brief and instant is the mantra everywhere.

Attention seems to be a relic of the past, incompatible with today's technological possibilities. Focus—what was it again? Wikipedia knows the answer:

Attention is the behavioural and cognitive process of selectively concentrating on a discrete aspect of information, whether deemed subjective or objective, while ignoring other perceivable information.

How long do you manage to selectively concentrate on a discrete aspect of information? To what extent are you able to focus on your current task? How long can you ignore other perceivable information? Are you able to concentrate at all, or do you fall victim to any distraction? How long can you keep up your level of attention?

Turn your attention to your goals, to the tasks that help you achieve these goals, to your selling strength, and your drivers of success. Pay particular attention to your 20 percent and make sure it happens in an automated way.

HAVE YOU RUNG IN YOUR MANUFACTURING AGE?

> Each of us is a king in our profession.
> —From the Arabic language

SPLITTING YOUR CRAFTS AND TASKS

With regard to standard practices, it does not matter much whether you work alone as a salesperson or run a larger business. In both cases, systemizing your work pays off enormously. There is a difference, though. If you work alone, it's just a matter of your personal habits and self-management capabilities. Once there are people working for you, success will depend not only on you but also on them. Don't rush, however, to blame failure on your people. Remember, a fish rots from the head down.

Let us make a huge jump backwards together. In fact, let's seemingly leave our topic and move several centuries back. The transition from handicrafts to manufacturing took place in the early modern period with the advent of manufactories producing goods like silk or playing cards. The famous Meissen porcelain manufactory, for instance, was established in 1710.

At that time, two variations of manufacturing appeared:

- Several crafts united under a common roof to work towards a common goal that benefited each of them.
- One craft was split into several sub-disciplines, and the craft's activities were divided into many sub-steps, each requiring highly specialized expertise.

Both variations aimed at a division of labour, to ultimately form a harmonious whole. The basic idea was to increase productivity. The manufacturing age wasn't of course the end of the story. With regard to technological, and particularly to societal development, it was only an intermediate phase, ultimately leading to the industrialization of work. Indeed, the reorganization of work processes helped enhance efficiency, reduce costs and increase profits. Various initial wrongs have been remedied over the years by legal provisions and social developments.

Let's return to our topic. Your business is also divided into various divisions of labour, each with its own tasks. As to sales, there are essentially three such divisions:

- Scheduling
- Selling
- Customer care

There are several other areas and tasks that may be added to these, of course. All tasks are best carried out in a focused manner, and so it would seem quite natural that the person or department responsible for scheduling a task is more likely to perform it most reliably, compared to someone who also has various other tasks to perform. Ideally, the individual performing the task should have the necessary expertise and inclination for it.

The manufacturing age ended long since. Business owners and salespeople may nevertheless ask the following questions:

- Did you subdivide your operational and selling activities?
- As a business owner, did you assign your best people to each of the tasks? As a salesperson, did you allocate your various tasks to the most appropriate hours of the day?
- Did you draw a clear distinction between the operational and selling procedures within your business, to make doubly sure that operations do not suppress sales?
- Are the people assigned to sales within your business in a position to invest all of their energies into sales activities without being distracted and impeded by other duties?
- As a business owner or salesperson, do you rigorously avoid selling yourself short by not taking care of the wrong tasks?

These questions are essentially the same for the individual salesperson, with the difference that there are no people to delegate the tasks to. You may, however, outsource tasks to external service providers. Moreover, you may define time windows to focus on certain areas such as scheduling, conducting sales talks, etc. Ideally, as in the case of people working for you, these tasks are best performed using predefined procedures and standard practices. You need, of course, clear and consistent self-management in order to define exactly when you will focus uninterruptedly on your selling activities.

For business owners, it is all about allocating tasks to the right people. For salespeople, it is all about scheduling tasks at appropriate hours of the day. Even if it dates back several centuries, have you rung in your own manufacturing age yet?

HOW TO DELIBERATELY ENGAGE YOUR PEOPLE

> A boss is not the one who does something but
> the one who raises the desire to do something.
> —Edgard Pisani

MOTIVATING FOR CHANGE AND NEW PROCEDURES

Let us take a look at your "team", if you have one. If you work alone
without a team, the following remarks may nevertheless be of interest to
you. After all, increasing your workforce may eventually become an option.
If you are already working with people you may say, "Well, if I worked
alone, it would be easy to always proceed systematically. I certainly would
implement many of these ideas. But how do I get my people to do so?"

Successfully implementing new behaviours and sustainably establishing
new, systematic approaches has a lot to do with old habits: yours as well as
those of your people. For a change to really take effect, some preconditions
need to be fulfilled for its implementation:

1. HAVE AND PROVIDE LONG-TERM ORIENTATION

Are you clear about your goals? Do they really motivate you? Your vision is what
keeps you going. Invest the time to communicate it to your people. Remember,
when introducing the concept of establishing standard practices, I asked
you, "Who exactly is your customer?" It's for them that you are establishing
standard practices in order to be more successful, professional and efficient.

Where is your business heading? The quest for change may lead us to
"chase another pig through the village" every now and then. Your people
know that in time the idea will fall into oblivion again and things will calm
down. Just sit it out until another pig comes running along, and wait until
that too disappears! Make sure your changes form an essential part of the
long-term orientation of your business.

2. COMMUNICATE CONVINCING REASONS FOR NEW PROCEDURES

It takes a lot of effort to establish new habits. Why change your behaviour if there is no need to? Without convincing reasons, a new approach will fail. What would be the result of going on as before? Describe to your people what else is likely to happen. Explain existing necessities, but don't play with feelings of fear. It is all about moving on together. Fear would have a paralyzing effect.

It is your job to illustrate why something is inevitable. Your people need to understand the reasons. Whatever you do must have a purpose. Change also needs a purpose. That is what this is all about.

3. FOCUS ON SOME POINTS

If reading this book or the blog www.ritterblog.de prompts you to ask yourself from time to time: "So, what else do I have to pay attention to?" my advice is, don't hurry. You can't make grass grow by pulling on it, nor can you introduce a whole new set of behaviours in one go.

Neither your people, nor you for that matter, are machines that can be reprogrammed simply by pushing a button. Proceed step by step. Sustainable changes need time, they must happen gradually. New things require concentration and deliberate action.

Nobody is capable of focusing equally on ten things at a time. Instead, focus on a few things, maybe just a first step towards systemizing. Even if you could do more right now, you should not.

4. DEFINE RESPONSIBILITIES

Who, apart from you, is responsible for making things happen? It is not enough to just outline a new endeavour. A statement like "it would be great if we could proceed like that in the future" sounds nice almost to the degree of complete meaninglessness. The term "responsibility" refers, among other things, to who exactly has to "respond" if something goes wrong.

Make things clear. Your people deserve it. Being responsible means being important. Engage your people in making your sales activities a success. Give importance to your people by delegating responsibility to them.

5. ENSURE CAPABILITY

All of the above is meaningless if your people lack the necessary capabilities. In that case, vision, reason, focus, and responsibility are to no avail. It is not enough for your people to know the new procedures, they must also be able to master them. Making sure they do is part of your job. At any rate, it makes a lot of sense to think about and work on it.

You are best off deploying your people in full accordance with their strengths and capabilities. That is your job as the business owner. There is no sense, for instance, in delegating the scheduling work to someone who tends to be a poor communicator. Choose the right people for the right task, and give them the help they need.

6. INVOLVE YOUR PEOPLE

You are of course in a position to decide what direction your business should take: for instance, moving from turning right to turning left, or from "what can I do for you?" to "let's make an appointment." Whether that makes sense may be controversial. However, as long as your people aren't convinced they will not be fully committed—they will not be committed at all, for that matter. There'll be no shortage of clever excuses ...

Involve your people. The more ideas they contribute, the more your approach becomes a joint approach. One-way communication isn't fashionable any more.

7. TAKE CONCERNS SERIOUSLY

Changes lead away from the familiar. People often fear they may not be able to cope with the new approach. Is it that your people are willing but unable to cope? Do they just believe they couldn't cope? Such concerns may get in the way of successful implementation. They form an insurmountable obstacle. To be able to eliminate them, you must be aware of them in the first place. So be alert. Your people will react, but you must listen carefully to intercept their subtle messages.

8. ASSIST YOUR PEOPLE

Changes have been jointly worked out, doubts have been dispelled, abilities have been developed, so here you go. Don't take your leave yet. New things tend to peter out in the initial phase, as old habits resurface with each action to launch an attack on the still unaccustomed methods. Assistance is particularly crucial during this time.

In the initial phase of a process of change, it is your job to be especially vigilant. Your new procedures are like a new set of game rules. Whose job is it to make sure that they are observed? Whose job is it to help people follow the new rules and procedures even if it is sometimes hard amid the daily stress? That's right, it's your job.

9. DON'T GET IN THE WAY OF YOUR PEOPLE

In a short time, new changes may overwhelm your people, if procedures are still in the initial familiarization phase and daily business is demanding full commitment. You know that your people currently need to focus on activities A and/or B, however, you swamp them with additional tasks C, D, E, F, and G. Someone has to do it, after all. Your people almost can't breathe anymore.

In this situation, how can new procedures turn into habits when your people are so pressed? It would be much easier for them to go on as before. The more your people feel overwhelmed, the more they will take the route of minimal effort. So start your change process with moderation. Introduce your new procedures in a considerate manner.

10. RECOGNIZE AND APPRECIATE PROGRESS

Things are under way. Your people start to produce results by working in a new way. The new system is taking effect. Do you recognize this initial progress, or do you just think, "That's what my people are paid for after all"?

Be sure to appreciate positive results in the initial phase; firstly, because it is only proper when appraising considerate collaboration, and secondly, in order to reinforce the new behaviour and to establish it step by step. Catch your people in the successful act and praise them. Do it, however, with moderation, or else it will have the opposite effect.

11. CONSCIOUSLY WORK ON YOUR PROCEDURES

It is not enough for you to ponder how to proceed with your business, perhaps whilst reading a book. Instead, write it down in 27 steps, and distribute it to your people. Developing your sales business means working on your procedures all of the time not—just for a couple of days or a weekend here and there.

Developing your business and your sales activities is like a game, with rules. The game goes on as long as the business exists. During this time, someone has to watch over the rules. That person is you. It is your job to make sure your standards are met. It is your job to make sure that things work out.

MOVING FROM UNCONSCIOUS TO CONSCIOUS QUALITY

> Stick to the meaning, and the words will take
> care of themselves.
> —Marcus Porcius Cato the Elder

AN ATTEMPT AT AN EXCURSION INTO PSYCHOLOGY

One part of developmental psychology is the concept of the so-called four competence stages. These describe the development of the initially incompetent individual into the resultant competent individual. This development comprises a total of four stages. I will describe them here in simple words:

- **Stage 1: Unconscious incompetence**
  At this first stage, an individual doesn't know what it is all about. The individual isn't aware of their potential area of activity and their deficits.
- **Stage 2: Conscious incompetence**
  At this second stage, an individual recognizes their own deficits. However, they don't know how to eliminate them. They aren't particularly eager to do something about it. Instead, they perceive and accept their own incompetence.
- **Stage 3: Conscious competence**
  At this stage, the individual has developed some skills. They have the necessary knowledge and abilities. Yet they still need to consciously focus on what they do in order to do it properly.
- **Stage 4: Unconscious competence**
  After frequently applying knowledge and abilities and consciously repeating certain actions for some time, an individual is now able to recall and use knowledge and abilities without much effort and focusing more or less automatically.

Standard practices and automatisms in your work, business or sales activities are subject to the same four stages. You may recognize yourself in one of the following stages:

- **Stage 1: Unconscious incompetence**
  In the work context, almost everything happens intuitively, always individually and with extreme time consumption. Nothing is known of the enormous benefits that standardization, systemization and unification of tasks and procedures may have.
- **Stage 2: Conscious incompetence**
  There is an awareness that reinventing the wheel all over again is time-consuming and not always economical. However, the status quo is tolerated. The necessary learning and growth process may temporarily lead to a feeling of being unable to cope.
- **Stage 3: Conscious competence**
  The awareness that standard systems and practices simplify tasks and effectively help individuals achieve their goals leads to their being introduced. Checklists and systems are put in place. However, as the old habits of acting unsystematically and intuitively are still deeply entrenched, an individual has to consciously focus on what they are doing in order to succeed. Without the constant effort of consciously focusing, the old intuitive habits easily sneak back in.
- **Stage 4: Unconscious competence**
  Standard practices and systems have become true automatisms. Without the need for conscious focus, the salesperson can now put mundane tasks on autopilot. The business owner is able to integrate important business processes into a unified system. For those involved, there is now no need to be constantly focused.

NEW HABITS NEED AWARENESS

Where are you right now? Surely there are tasks and procedures in which you have made some progress already. With others, the process of systemizing has only just begun. Pay attention to the fact that only by establishing new habits can old patterns of behaviour be replaced.

Moreover, consider that success is reached step by step. Start with a task that has to be systemized, and move on to competence stage 4 by introducing a new sales-promoting and simplifying procedure. Only then should you proceed to the next task. Concerning the previous task, stay alert for a while so as not to fall back into the old patterns of behaviour. Work on your service quality, and develop first-class procedures and habits. The more often you repeat a new procedure, the sooner it will turn into a familiar pattern. There is no better catalyst for your business and sales success than habits that let you achieve your goals automatically. It is exactly these habits that help you automate your business and your sales activities.

AT THE CEMETERY OF YOUR INTENTIONS

> Don't try to take too many steps at a time ...
> Someone who has a long road in front of her
> doesn't run.
> —Paula Modersohn-Becker

IF IT WASN'T IMPORTANT ENOUGH

Many business owners and salespeople want to develop their business, simplify their procedures, and increase their sales success. They always look for motivational input, read a book, undergo training, and engage a consultancy. Then they come to the implementation—at least theoretically. In reality, there is a long to-do list with lots of other tasks waiting to be taken care of. Whilst the motivation to change things may have been paramount at the beginning, it gradually, and often quite rapidly, fades away. At the same time, the reasons why the intended changes can't be successfully implemented miraculously proliferate. "The circumstances simply aren't favourable." "We should have known right from the beginning." "It was just a theory."

What was the last endeavour that you failed to carry through? What did you want to implement, after all? What did you want to change? Why haven't you implemented it? Why has it ended up on the scrapheap of your unfulfilled dreams, in the cemetery of your endeavours, stuck on the runway of your high-flying plans?

From my point of view, the answer is quite simple. Here it is again. You didn't deem it important. You didn't deem it important enough. At least, there were other things you deemed more important. It was easier for you not to implement it. You couldn't prevent the old ways and the old habits from getting hold of you again. You didn't burn to implement the new and better ways. At best, it had been only a tiny little flame.

During the last two decades or so, I have met with many very successful business owners and salespeople. They all had one thing in common. Instead of just planning to do things, they actually did them. They did and do realize their plans, with a passion. They didn't allow various adversities to distract them, or to prevent them from doing what they were committed to do. Often, they could see the results of their endeavours before their mind's eye long before they actually realized them. They travelled into the future to experience and enjoy the results of their changes.

There are countless people who make all sorts of plans, and still more plans. Each time they have made a plan, they then look for reasons why it is impossible to realize it. For years they refuse to move forward by laying the blame on the environment and the circumstances. There was simply no way to do it. What a pity.

SHOW BUSINESS ACUMEN

All you need to do is to act consistently. It is essential that you walk your talk, and do what you say you want to do. Acting in this way will have its consequences—as does failing to do so.

As we often see in our training and consulting activities and during other events, the ability to act consistently is one of the main drivers of success. Such consistent action includes clarity and focusing on what is most important by concentrating on a limited set of priorities that are manageable and feasible.

Additionally, you need awareness and focus. Decide first whether something is important to you. As soon as you are sure, stay focused on it. Make a note of your commitments, put them on your desk, and don't get distracted. Don't undertake to do too many things at a time. If in doubt, limit yourself to one or two steps, and start with the most important. The rest may come later. Ideally choose your first steps in such a way that a first small success can be quickly achieved, thereby enhancing your motivation to go on. Involve others by talking about it, and commit to your plans by communicating them. Use any help available.

Sticking to it, acting consistently, and staying focused—that is your job. And if it is important to you, I bet you will be up to it.

YET ANOTHER SMALL EXAMPLE

I don't have rituals—except for those things I do
the same way over and over again.
—Michael Ballack

DO YOU KNOW HANS WURST?

Do you know Hans Wurst? Before we reach the end of this book, let us
talk about his genuine Thüringer Rostbratwurst. As this may be somewhat
unexpected, I'll give you a short explanation. On days when I'm not out
lecturing but "home" in the Institut Ritter, a question arises as to what
kind of lunch I should get myself. Our institute doesn't have a canteen.
However, there are quite a few options available in the neighbourhood.
Sometimes, especially if time is limited, I choose a simple local offering, a
genuine Thüringer from Hans Wurst.

Well, what does a sausage stand have to do with our topic? I could equally
write about an Italian restaurant just opposite our institute, a Greek
restaurant not far from it, the inevitable Rathskeller, a fish restaurant
around the corner, a professional sandwich-&-more shop etc. So why Hans
Wurst? The answer is quite simple. From my point of view, seen through
the spectacles of the notorious consultant, Hans Wurst beats them all.

Why does he? That's an easy one, too. Hans Wurst has a clear product range.
Anyone who comes to him is looking for—and finds—the best Thuringian
sausage available. Where it comes to the goods offered, he is clearly positioned.
However, that is not the point, as he is not the only one who can do this. What is
truly unique is that no matter when you visit his stand directly besides St. Jacobs
in Sangerhausen (no more than two minutes' walk from my desk), no matter
what mood he or you are in, the questions asked and the answers given are
always exactly the same. I'll write them down for you. You line up, or maybe you
are lucky and there is no big crowd. Either way, you are soon standing in front
of the grill, and there they are, the bronzed genuine Thüringers. Here we go:

- **Which one would you like?**
  The start is very customer-friendly. You can take a pleasant look at the grill and decide which Thuringian most appeals to you. A dark, almost black one, or a pale one? Tastes differ ...
- **Mustard, ketchup, or both?**
  Once you have made your choice and the sausage is packed in its roll, you may choose your sauce. There is a clear choice, though it's rather unusual to be offered both at a time ...
- **Coffee for free?**
  Now, this tops it all. With the sausage wrapped up, it's time for a freebie. There is no better way to close a deal than with a present. Whether or not a coffee sounds alluring to you, the offer makes you feel good. The next thing is EUR 1.80, the current rate for a Thüringer in Sangerhausen. Elsewhere in the region, you may only get half a sausage for the same price.

These three questions are invariably asked. The quality of the process is guaranteed, no matter who happens to man the stand. By the way, there are customers around at all times of the day. Some just eat their Thüringers and leave, while those who opted for the coffee often stay a bit longer. That is a good way to promote customer loyalty, and where there is a crowd, others feel tempted to join in.

From a consultant's point of view, Hans Wurst does a lot of things right:

- There is a clear product range, so the customer knows what they are getting.
- The customer is competently involved in the decision process.
- There is an initial special, the possibility of two sauces at a time.
- Unexpectedly and for free, there is a second special crowning the deal.
- The process is simple, clearly defined and easy to delegate.

The whole process is so simple that I can describe it here for you. Although this is not laid down in the system, it usually ends with a friendly "see you tomorrow", which is certainly true in many cases.

Now you may think, "there is quite a difference between selling sausages and my business and sales activities." You are right. The point, however, is that there is a clear standard, a predetermined system, which is exactly what this book is all about. Each of your work processes needs a system that is realized over and over again. The quality of your business and the quality of your sales activities ultimately depends on the quality of your systems, and it is your job to sustainably establish them.

Your systems should reinforce your sales processes and professionalize your customer service. You should also think about how to give your business a design so simple and straightforward that each of your people is able to perform with the same quality, even if only a very short period of familiarization is given.

Even if you have rather more systems than Hans Wurst, the basic principle is the same. By the way, even my youngest son Johannes (14) swears by Hans Wurst ...

EPILOGUE

WHAT SKIING AND YOUR BUSINESS HAVE IN COMMON

> Your task is not to foresee the future, but to
> enable it.
> —Antoine de Saint-Exupéry

Having thought so much about systemizing and standardizing, a week I spent in Austria more than twenty years ago comes to mind. That was quite a while back. It was in 1991, in Tyrol ...

For someone who has grown up in the lowlands, learning to ski as a child is not a matter of course. While children born in the Alpine region are naturally familiar with skis as a means of transportation, I had never been put on skis at an early age. I wasn't used to these two planks—I was rather like some people who don't learn to swim.

In 1991, I finally wanted to remedy this shortcoming. The endeavour brought me to Sölden where I participated in a standard skiing course—one for beginners, of course. Not knowing what was in store for me, I wasn't nervous. Aren't they all supposed to be beginners? I could even be the one-eyed man among the blind, I thought.

Events did not transpire quite as I expected, however. My group consisted entirely of women of an advanced age. I had the feeling that there was at least a generation between us. In short, I was the spring chicken of the group. Compared to everybody else, I was completely ignorant. Everybody beat me, at least where it came to skiing skills. Who would have expected it? They were certainly not beginners. They simply didn't want to make fools of themselves.

This was my role throughout the whole of Monday. It was so frustrating that on Tuesday, the second day of the skiing course, I stayed clear of my group. I just wanted to practice somewhere, alone, and so I did. While my group had their lessons in the upper regions, I stayed near the village.

After some hours, I mastered some combinations of movement which enabled me to remain upright for quite some time without having too much close contact with the snow. Successes then followed. Still, a live recording of my attempts at that time would certainly be a YouTube hit nowadays ...

The next day, Wednesday, feeling motivated and invigorated, I had the courage to return to the group. They had worried about me and welcomed me back. So I learned and skied and learned and skied on various slopes until Friday. As for my performance, I was now in midfield, the highest I could possibly aspire to. It was my first and my last skiing course. Today my skiing skills are about the same as they were at that time. Maybe I have improved a little bit. But learning to ski has never been a priority to me since then.

Every now and again, I will ski. Not really well, but not too badly either. I even manage to descend black slopes without falling. Experts watching me do however notice my various shortcomings. Moreover, I have a problem. After several descents, I get tired and need a break. This is the tell-tale sign that I have never really learned how to ski. When I ski, I use a lot of force and a little technique. In fact, there is virtually no technique at all. For me, it is simply a matter of getting down the hill, never mind how.

So, why am I writing all this? Many business owners and salespeople also rely on force rather than technique to run their businesses. The more work there is, the more energy and time they invest, again and again. Inevitably, there comes a point where there is simply no more energy and time left to invest. From an ecological perspective, those who do so will consume their whole energy. When I ski, a little break is enough for me to recover my breath. Business owners and salespeople potentially need much longer breaks, depending on how far they have exhausted their batteries.

Create systematic procedures. Develop automatisms. Work on your standard practices and simplify whatever you do. Whatever you standardize will no longer cost you effort of thought. It will run subconsciously and almost automatically. Use the examples of this book. Consider it a great opportunity to develop your skills.

Also, work on your technique. Lead your business or perform your sales activities in a better way than I ski. Although this doesn't sound too ambitious, that just makes it all the more important.

Make sure your business and your sales activities run "automatically" in the best possible sense. Selling can run smoothly. Sales can run automatically.

APPENDICES

A1. SELF-ASSESSMENT OF THE SALES SYSTEMS DESCRIBED IN THIS BOOK

Consciously assess the following systems of sustainable selling success using a scale from 1 to 6 where 1 = excellent and 6 = failing.

System	1	2	3	4	5	6
1. How systematically do others become aware of you?						
2. How systematically do others campaign for you?						
3. How systematically do you convert potentials into customers?						
4. How systematically do you contact your customers by letter?						
5. How systematically do you categorize your customers?						
6. How systematically do your class C customers generate profit?						
7. How systematically do you service your class A customers?						
8. How systematically do you develop your potential customers?						
9. How systematically do you follow up?						
10. How systematically do you continue to create value for your customers?						

System	1	2	3	4	5	6
11. How systematically do your customers recommend you to others?						
12. How systematically do you offer extras to your customers?						
13. How systematically do you deal with customer defection?						

A2. POSSIBLE WAYS TO EMBED SUCH SYSTEMS IN YOUR DAY-TO-DAY SALES OPERATIONS

How systematically do you currently perform in your daily business and sales activities? There are a variety of ways to put your standard practices on record.

Systems and procedures can be described in shorthand step by step. From this, a manual can be derived. Processes can be filmed and posted on an internal YouTube channel. Camtasia screen recordings can help to document the use of certain computer applications, showing, for instance, where you have to click and in which order to get a certain result.

The following brief check helps you to determine which processes you are already using or planning to use for your further development.

Possible ways to embed systems and practices in your work routine	I'm already using it	I plan to use it	Not applicable
Checklists (printed)			
Checklists (PDF)			
Predetermined course of sales talk			
Consulting folders with identical structure			
Phone call guides for various purposes			
Face-to-face talk guides for various purposes			
Predetermined course for after-sales service			
Course of action for each customer class			

Possible ways to embed systems and practices in your work routine	I'm already using it	I plan to use it	Not applicable
Course of action for dealing with people			
Manual on your sales approaches			
Manual on your guaranteed customer service offerings			
Online manual, technically realized as a "Wiki"			
YouTube videos as an alternative to text-based descriptions			
Camtasia screen videos on computer issues			

A3. POSSIBLE WAYS TO INCREASE THE VISIBILITY OF YOUR BUSINESS

Consider which of the following examples suit your industry, your sales activities and your circumstances. If possible, determine a deadline for the realization (D) and—if appropriate—a person responsible (R).

Some possible ways to make yourself more visible	Good idea		I'm already doing it	Not applicable
	D	R		
Organize smaller or bigger events for your community/ target group				
Do something for your community/target group to draw media attention				
Get featured in a newspaper				
Write an interesting column for a newspaper				
Launch an award for your target group				
Publish a magazine for your community/target group				
Deliver attention-grabbing presentations at meetings				
Include regional and national celebrities				
Use crazy actions to spice up your image				

A4. POSSIBLE WAYS TO CARE FOR YOUR CLASS A CUSTOMERS

Consider which of the following examples suit your industry and your customer care. If possible, determine a deadline for the realization (D) and—if appropriate—a responsible person (R).

Some possible ways to provide certain customers with special customer care	Good idea		I'm already doing it	Not applicable
	D	R		
Send newsletters (hard-copy or e-mail) quarterly, for instance				
Reach out to customers giving them "huddle calls" at fixed intervals				
Stage a worthwhile unusual annual event exclusively for class A customers				
Cross-link your class A customers to (unselfishly) promote their business				
Offer preferential service by providing longer hours of accessibility/special hotline				
Improve cost-benefit ratio by offering extensive collaboration				
Pay special attention once a year, not necessarily in a holiday season				
Offer clearly defined 360-degree care, possibly including unusual additional service				

Some possible ways to provide certain customers with special customer care	Good idea		I'm already doing it	Not applicable
	D	R		
Ask customers individually about their satisfaction, their needs and wishes				
Offer special care as a service guaranteed in writing (a certificate, for instance)				
Offer special information via a separate log-in on your homepage				
Make special customer status "tangible" by handing out a golden customer card, for instance				

ABOUT THE AUTHOR

The most important lever for sustainable sales success? Systems, systems, systems. Only the right habits turn fair-weather sellers into all-time sellers.
—Steffen Ritter

Steffen Ritter is one of the best-known speakers on business and sales topics in the German-speaking regions. He is considered Germany's leading consultant for financial service providers, insurers, sellers, and agents.

For more than two decades he has been an advocate and promoter of professionalizing sales activities. He has launched several well-regarded awards. Steffen Ritter, multiple bestselling author and, since 1999, editor of his own magazine "Unternehmer-Ass", is himself a passionate entrepreneur. As a keynote speaker at congresses and meetings, as well as in his annual workshop "BEST OF Vertrieb", he enthrals, motivates and enthuses his audience with his fine sense of humour, linguistic finesse, and numerous "aha" moments.

Since 1992, Steffen Ritter has been managing director and mastermind of the consulting and training firm "Institut Ritter". He is a partner and managing director of the "Institut für Versicherungsvertrieb Beratungsgesellschaft mbH". In a broad range of largely modularly organized training units, his firms' coaches and consultants accompany sellers on their journey from founding a business to turning it into a big and profitable company. Since 2005, Steffen Ritter has run "Development Days" at Cape Arkona on the island Rügen and near the Zugspitze in the Alps. He can be booked for highlight trainings and annual meetings. Additionally, he offers a limited number of open seminars, in which he inspires his audience by addressing them in his distinctive humorous and charismatic way.

For more comprehensive information about the Institut Ritter, please visit www.institutritter.de or the YouTube channel www.youtube.com/steffenritterlive.

If you are a member of Facebook, you can experience the Institut Ritter firsthand on www.facebook.com/institutritter, or subscribe to Steffen Ritter on www.facebook.com/steffenritterlive.

Contact Steffen Ritter:

c/o Institut Ritter GmbH
Markt 5
D-06526 Sangerhausen

Telephone: +49 (0) 3464 573980
E-mail: info@institutritter.de
Telefax: +49 (0) 3464 573982
Internet: www.institutritter.de

INDEX

GABAL global

English Editions by GABAL Publishing

Who We Are

GABAL provides proven practical knowledge and publishes media products on the topics of business, success, and life. With over 600 experienced, international authors from various industries and education, we inspire businesses and people to move forward.

GABAL. Your publisher.
Motivating. Sympathetic. Pragmatic.

These three adjectives describe the core brand of GABAL. They describe how we think, feel, and work. They describe the style and mission of our books and media. GABAL is your publisher, because we want to bring you forward. Not with finger-pointing, not divorced from reality, not pointy-headed or purely academic, but motivating in effect, sympathetic in appearance, and pragmatically-oriented toward results.

Our books have only one concern: they want to help the reader improve. In business. For success. In life.

Our target reader
People who want to develop personally and/or professionally

As a modern media house GABAL publishes books, audio books, and e-books for people and companies that want to develop further. Our books are aimed at people who are looking for knowledge about current issues in business and education that can be put into practice quickly.

For more information, see the GABAL global website:

http://www.iuniverse.com/Packages/GABAL-Global-Editions.aspx

Printed in the United States
By Bookmasters